Dr Sue Chadwick is a Strategic Planning Advisor with Pinsent Masons and Chair of the Housing Project Group at Cambridge Ahead. She has more than 25 years experience as a planning lawyer including working for a range of County and District authorities, two London Boroughs, and a number of years at Herbert Smith Freehills. She has taught planning law and policy at Cambridge University, has a PhD on the meaning and interpretation of sustainable development in the planning framework and currently delivers training for MBL seminars and LLG Legal Training.

Resolutions and Reasons: A Practical Guide to Decision Making in Planning

Resolutions and Reasons: A Practical Guide to Decision Making in Planning

Dr Sue Chadwick
Solicitor

Law Brief Publishing

Published 2019 by Law Brief Publishing, an imprint of Law Brief Publishing Ltd
30 The Parks
Minehead
Somerset
TA24 8BT

www.lawbriefpublishing.com

Paperback: 978-1-911035-91-6

PREFACE

It is more than 30 years since I first gave advice to a planning committee, but I still remember how terrifying the experience was. Over the years knowledge and experience reduced the fear but advising committees remained challenging.

Part of the reason for this was that, even when I became familiar with planning law, the governance context was still challenging and there was little in the textbooks to deal with that.

This book aims to provide basic information on planning decisions and their context in local government decision making generally. It is aimed at anyone who wants or needs a working knowledge not just of the law but how that law is applied in practical way and in the wider governance context. Some knowledge of the system will be helpful but not essential and even the most experienced practitioner may benefit from some of the governance topics covered. If it helps just one planning lawyer, planner or newly elected councillor then it will have done its job.

Writing this book has, generally, been a pleasure as well as a learning experience, due in no small part to support from Pinsent Masons LLP, my current employer and in particular my colleague Anna Coyle who invested her time and considerable intellect in helping me with the content and structure of chapters 1 and 2.

The stated law and policy is, to the best of my knowledge, correct and up-to-date as at 1st May 2019.

Sue Chadwick
May 2019

CONTENTS

INTRODUCTION

For most people 1997 will be noted for the birth of Marcus Rashford, and Dolly the sheep; the death of Princess Diana, the launch of Channel 5, and a general election that saw Tony Blair celebrate his election with a 'Cool Britannia' reception at Downing Street attended by Noel Gallagher, Vivienne Westwood and Helen Mirren. For a few planning lawyers it is also the year the House of Lords issued the *City of Edinburgh*[1] judgment on how planning decisions should be made.

In 2019 Marcus Rashford lights up the pitch at Old Trafford, Dolly is dead, Diana's children have children, Cool has been replaced by Woke – and Brittannia is neither – but the issues considered in *City of Edinburgh* are still highly relevant to the English planning system. The primary purpose of this book is to explore and explain the law, policy and governance issues that surround the exercise of the two statutory provisions ("the legal test") that sit at the heart of the planning decision making process in 2019:

- Section 70(2) of the Town and Country Planning Act 1990 ("the 1990 Act") which provides that "in dealing with an application for planning permission... the authority shall have regard to the provisions of the development, so far as material to the application, and to any other material considerations" the decision-maker shall have regard to the provisions of the development plan, so far as material to the application.

1 City of Edinburgh Council v Secretary of State for Scotland 1998 SC (HL) 33

- Section 38(6) of the Planning and Compulsory Purchase Act 2004 ("the 2004 Act") which provides that "If regard is to be had to the development plan for the purpose of any determination to be made under the planning Acts, the determination must be made in accordance with the plan unless material considerations indicate otherwise."

The book will focus on the legal test set out above, beginning with the meaning and effect of the development plan, moving on to the scope of material considerations and how they are balanced against the plan in the decision making process. It will also look in detail at how this traditional balance shifted with the adoption of the National Planning Policy Framework 2012, the introduction of the 'tilted balance' presumption in favour of sustainable development, and its impact in cases such as 'Suffolk Coastal'.

Planning decisions are at risk of being quashed for both legal and procedural errors. The book will therefore additionally examine other wider planning considerations that may be relevant such as the specific legal duties relating to the consideration of sites that contain listed buildings and conservation areas or are affected by landscape or ecological designations. And as even the hardest of Brexit exits will not immediately wipe out the impact of European issues such as Environmental Impact Assessments and Habitat Regulations assessments so these issues, along with obligations arising from the Human Rights Act 2001 and the Equality Act 2010 will be summarised, with reference to the most recent caselaw.

Planning applications are submitted by individuals who own or want to develop land but they are decided by local authorities and the decision making process is a public function. This means that governance issues are relevant, such as the content and relevance of the Council's constitution including the scheme of delegation, the difference between regulatory and Executive functions, member codes, interests and bias, committee reports and minutes and the latest position on reasons – for approvals and refusals. The book will examine all of these issues with reference to planning decisions.

CHAPTER ONE
THE PLAN AND THE PLANNING BALANCE

The traditional planning balance

The current version of the legal test is an awkward conflation of two separate pieces of legislation: Section 70(2) of the 1990 Act and Section 38 (6) of the 2004 Act. They are a deceptively simple legal scaffold for a complex balancing process involving law, policy and a range of other socio-political considerations. The most comprehensive explanation of the process was provided by the Supreme Court in 1997, in the *City of Edinburgh* case mentioned above:

> "*In the practical application of section 18A it will obviously be necessary for the decision-maker to consider the development plan, identify any provisions in it which are relevant to the question before him and make a proper interpretation of them. His decision will be open to challenge if he fails to have regard to a policy in the development plan which is relevant to the application or fails properly to interpret it. He will also have to consider whether the development proposed in the application before him does or does not accord with the development plan. There may be some points in the plan which support the proposal but there may be some considerations pointing in the opposite direction. He will require to assess all of these and then decide whether in light of the whole plan the proposal does or does not accord with it. He will also have to identify all the other material considerations which are relevant to the application and to which he should have regard. He will then have to note which of them support the application and*

which of them do not, and he will have to assess the weight to be given to all of these considerations. He will have to decide whether there are considerations of such weight as to indicate that the development plan should not be accorded the priority which the statute has given to it. And having weighed these considerations and determined these matters he will require to form his opinion on the disposal of the application. If he fails to take account of some material consideration or takes account of some consideration which is irrelevant to the application his decision will be open to challenge. But the assessment of the considerations can only be challenged on the ground that it is irrational or perverse."

The principles were approved by the Supreme Court in 2012[1] and continue to be referred to in ongoing case law[2] The decision maker must therefore: 1) identify the development plan; 2) identify the policies in it relevant to the development and whether or not the proposal 'accords' with it; 3) identify material considerations relevant to the development; and 4) assess the particular proposal under consideration in the light of both.

The development plan

Since town planning first became a matter of law, local authorities have had a power to create schemes or plans setting the framework for development in their area. For example the Town and Country Planning Act 1947 Act enabled each of the newly formed local planning authorities to survey its area and submit that survey to the Minister of Town and Country Planning with a "development plan",

1 Tesco Stores Limited v Dundee City Council 2012 UKSC 13

2 South Gloucestershire Council v Secretary of State for Housing, Communities And Local Government [2019] EWHC 181 (Admin)

indicating the manner in which they proposed that land in their area should be used. These schemes – referred to as the "development plan" in section 70 – are still formulated, assessed and adopted at a local level and set broad development aspirations and constraints for the area without being required to have regard to individual land ownership ambitions.

It is essential to know what the 'development plan is' if it is to be given the correct weight in the planning process. If a document has development plan status then it must be identified as such and given appropriate priority. If it is not then this will be a legal error putting the decision is at risk. Unfortunately it is not always easy to identify the development plan – and no single definition of what a development plan is either.

- Section 336 of the 1990 Planning Act states that "development plan" must be construed in accordance with section 38 of the 2004 Act;

- Section 38 (3)(b) of the 2004 Act states that "the development plan is…the development plan documents (taken as a whole) which have been adopted or approved in relation to that area"

- Section 37(3) of the 2004 which defines a development plan document ('DPD') as a local development document ('LDD') specified as a [DPD] in the local development scheme".

- Section 17(7) of the 2004 states that regulations may prescribe which descriptions of documents are DPDs;

- Regulation 2 of the Town and Country Planning (Local Planning) (England) Regulations 2012 ("the 2012 Regulations") defines "local plan" as "any document of the description referred to in regulation 5(1)(a)(i), (ii) or (iv) or 5(2)(a) or (b)

- The relevant criteria in Regulation 5 are

  - (1)(a) ... statements regarding one or more of the following - (i) the development and use of land which the local planning authority wish to encourage during any specified period; (ii) the allocation of sites for a particular development or use;...(iv) development management and site allocation policies, which are intended to guide the determination of applications for planning permission.

  - (2).. (a) any document which -(iii) contains the local planning authority's policies in relation to the area; .. (b) any other document which includes a site allocation policy.

In effect, when asking whether or not a particular document is, or is not, a 'development plan' for the purpose of the legal test the core question is not what it is called but whether or not it comes within the criteria established within a description referred to in regulation 5(1)(a)(i), (ii) or (iv), or 5(2)(a) or (b). The question whether a document falls within the definition of a "local plan", a "supplementary planning document" or neither definition requires the application of facts to the specific words of the regulations. Documents such as strategic or development management policies will generally be within the definition of a development plan and in London, the London Plan will always be part of the development plan. In the case of other documents such as local area plans, area action plans, supplementary planning guidance/documents and other strategic documents, affecting part of or the whole of an area things are more problematic, and it is not surprising therefore that the issue has come before the courts.

In *Skipton Properties Ltd*[3] Jay J wrestled with the definitions and commented that "the quest for the true construction and meaning of regulation 5(1)(a) is unnecessarily challenging. Frankly, those responsible for these regulations should consider redrafting them." This case, which considered whether a document about negotiating affordable housing contributions was required to be adopted as a development plan document. Jay eventually concluded (para 92) that the document contained "statements in the nature of policies which pertain to the development and use of land" so was an interim policy "in the nature of" a development plan document.

The defining characteristics of the development plan were also considered recently in the case of *McCarthy and Stone*[4] that considered the emerging supplementary planning guidance produced to support housing policies in the London Plan. One of the one of the contentions was that it was unlawful because it should have been consulted

---

3 Skipton Properties Ltd, R (On the Application Of) v Craven District Council [2017] EWHC 534 (Admin)

4 McCarthy and Stone Retirement Lifestyles Ltd & Ors, R (on the application of) v Greater London Authority [2018] EWHC 1202 (Admin)

and adopted as a London Plan policy. Ouseley J acknowledged that "There is no judicial guidance on what constitutes policy and what SPG" (para 26). He noted that "the line between guidance and policy is not a bright line, particularly when it comes to an assessment of the level of detail appropriate for a plan" (para 33) and though a court could decide whether or not a document should be in a spatial strategy there was still " considerable room for the Court to respect the plan-maker's judgment on what is to receive the weight of the development plan" (para 34). This is rather an unhelpful judgment in terms of determining what is DPD and what is not, and further arguments are likely in this area.

The Development Plan – Neighbourhood Plans

Where there is a neighbourhood plan this will always comprise part of the development plan, thanks to sections 38A and 38B of the 2004 Act.

- Section 38A states that a development plan is "a plan which sets out policies (however expressed) in relation to the development and use of land in the whole or any part of a particular neighbourhood area."

- Section 38B adds some detail as to what the neighbourhood plan must do, requiring that it must specify the period for which it is to have effect and may not include provisions about certain categories of excluded development or relate to more than one neighbourhood area. "Excluded" development is set out in new section 61K of the Town and Country Planning Act 1990 and includes 'County Matters' such as minerals and waste, large projects within Annex 1 of the

> Environmental Impact Assessment Directive (Council Directive 85/337/EEC) and Nationally Significant Infrastructure Projects. Section 38B also states that only one neighbourhood development plan may be made for each neighbourhood area.

Neighbourhood Plans are development plan documents but have their own legislative origins and are covered by different regulations. They are generated from, drafted by and consulted on – at least in the initial stages – by ordinary members of a local community rather than the established local authority and legal validity depends on compliance with the basic conditions set out in Schedule 4B of the Town and Country Planning Act 1990 rather than the more detailed concept of "soundness" applied to other development plan documents.

Criticised as creating "an uneven geography of representation in favour of the better educated, well-off and more vocal social groups"[5], they cover relatively small areas of land, but the scope of geographic coverage belies their overall influence. For an increasing number of local authorities, the policies contained in neighbourhood plans must both be taken into account and given equivalent status with the traditional development plan documents. One of the basic conditions that must be complied with is that the emerging neighbourhood plan should be in accordance with the adopted development plan, but where that plan is under review, strategic policies in neighbourhood plans can be effective in preventing development. Paragraph 30 of the Framework confirms that "Once a neighbourhood plan has been brought into force, the policies it con-

---

5 Simin Davoudi & Paul Cowie 'Are English Neighbourhood forums democratically legitimate?' Planning Theory and Practice Vol 1 No. 4 562

tains take precedence over existing non-strategic policies in a local plan covering the neighbourhood area" and in indeed in the 2017 *DLA Delivery*[6] case the Court of Appeal confirmed that an NDP could legitimately set a policy framework for development in its area even where there was no superior plan to be in conformity with.

The planning balance: presumption in favour of the development plan

Once the decision maker has identified the development plan, the next requirement of the legal test is to 'have regard' to its provisions where they are material to the application in hand. However, as recognised by Lord Reed in the 2012 *Tesco Stores* case, "development plans are full of broad statements of policy, many of which may be mutually irreconcilable".[7] Plans are so broad in scope that they can be used to create and present legitimate arguments both in favour of, and against, the proposal at hand. The decision maker must consider this wide and sometimes conflicting range of policy aims and ambitions, and decide whether or not a particular application is 'in accordance with' the plan.

The process is neither simple nor static, and may be made more complex where the 'development plan' comprises more than one document. In addition, the legal test requires not only that regard should be had to the relevant development plan policies but also that the decision should be made "in accordance with the plan unless material considerations indicate otherwise" – known as the pre-

---

6 DLA Delivery Ltd, R (On the Application Of) v Lewes District Council [2017] EWCA Civ 58

7 Tesco Stores Limited (Appellants) v Dundee City Council (Respondents) (Scotland) [2012] UKSC 13 [19]

sumption in favour of the development plan, introduced in 1991 as a late amendment to the Planning and Compensation Bill. Its status was confirmed by the *City of Edinburgh* case and Lord Clyde's ruling that: "...there is now a presumption that the development plan is to govern the decision on an application for planning permission". It was given statutory force by the enactment of section 38(6) of the 2004 Act.

The tilted balance: presumption in favour of sustainable development

The key national planning policy document is the 2019 National Planning Policy Framework but it is the predecessor document that introduced one of the most significant recent changes to the planning system. On 27 March 2012 a national planning policy framework was introduced with an immediate impact on all planning decisions. It included a "presumption in favour of sustainable development that is the basis for every plan, and every decision".

For the purposes of planning decisions, the key paragraphs were 6 and 14. Paragraph 6 stated that "The policies in paragraphs 18 to 219, taken as a whole, constitute the Government's view of what sustainable development in England means in practice for the planning system". This paragraph introduced a framework-specific definition that was ring-fenced by the content of the Framework itself. Paragraph 14 introduced a presumption ("the paragraph 14 presumption") in favour of sustainable development. When applied to planning applications paragraph 14 stated that

- sustainable development meant "approving development proposals that accord with the development plan without delay;

- Where the development plan is absent, silent or relevant policies were out-of-date, sustainable development meant "granting permission unless any adverse impacts of doing so would significantly and demonstrably outweigh the benefits, when assessed against the policies in this Framework taken as a whole; or specific policies in this Framework indicate development should be restricted."

The consequences of the intersection of paragraphs 6 and 14 were profound. In specific circumstances planning decision makers were now required, despite the established statutory presumption in favour of the development plan, to apply the Framework policies in preference to the development plan where it was "absent silent or out of date". In *Bloor Homes*[8] Lindblom J comprehensively explored and defined the circumstances in which the presumption might apply, ruling that:

- A development plan will be "absent" if none has been adopted for the relevant area;

- ...it may be "silent" because it lacks policy relevant to the project under consideration

- ...relevant policies...may have been overtaken by things that have happened since it was adopted...

---

8 Bloor Homes East Midlands Ltd v Secretary of State for Communities and Local Government & Anor [2014] EWHC 754 (Admin)

Labelling them as the 'three possible shortcomings' of a development plan, he was equally clear that any of them, if present, would impose a requirement, in the form of the presumption, that planning permission be granted.

The tilted balance and 'Suffolk Coastal'

For local authorities who wanted to retain strategic control over new development compliance with the Framework was essential – but difficult to achieve, especially in terms of housing supply, because of two more paragraphs in the 2012 Framework:

- Paragraph 49 of the Framework required that "relevant policies for the supply of housing" should not be considered "up-to-date", unless the authority could demonstrate a five-year supply of deliverable housing sites;

- Paragraph 47 set out what was required to demonstrate that the local authority had the required five-year supply.

The significance of these two paragraphs and their interrelationship with paragraph 14 was critical for local authorities seeking to preserve the status of their local development plans in the decision-making process. If the local authority had the required 5-year supply, the development plan policies would retain their dominance in the planning decision process and the traditional planning balance would apply. But where a local authority did not have the required supply of deliverable houses, paragraph 47 automatically rendered all of their plan 'policies for the supply of housing' automatically out of date, no matter how recently the plan was adopted, and required the application of the paragraph 14 presumption to be applied.

Where the local authority did not have the necessary 5-year supply of housing land, the meaning of "policies for the supply of housing" became increasingly important. Applicants promoting developments that were non-compliant with development plans wanted the phrase to be interpreted broadly and apply to as many policies as possible. Local authorities understandably argued for a narrow definition, limiting the damage that could be done to the development plan policies and their weight in the planning process. The scope of the phrase was not resolved until the Supreme Court ruling in the 'Suffolk Coastal' decision in May 2017.

The case had its origins in January 2013 when a developer – Hopkins Homes – submitted a proposal to Suffolk Coastal District Council for a residential development of 26 dwellings. The site was designated as historic parkland and the proposal conflicted with development plan policy SP29 which allowed new development only if it "of necessity requires to be located there". The Council refused permission, partly in reliance on SP29, and Hopkins Homes appealed the decision. If – as Hopkins Homes argued – policy SP29 was a 'policy for the supply of housing' then the absence of a five-year supply of housing land meant that it must be considered "out of date". If – as the Council argued – it was not, then it would retain its status as an up-to-date development plan policy. The planning inspector supported the Council's position, and refused permission for the development.

Hopkins Homes challenged that decision and were initially successful – in January 2015[9] Supperstone J ruled that policy SP29 was a policy for the supply of housing, that it did come within the scope

9 Hopkins Homes Ltd v Secretary of State for Communities And Local Government & Anor [2015] EWHC 132 (Admin)

of paragraph 49, and that the Inspector's misinterpretation was a legal defect. The original decision to refuse permission was quashed. However, within 4 weeks of this ruling another judge took a different view on the same issue.[10] This was another residential development in Cheshire, which was refused because it was in conflict with development plan policies including policy NE4 protecting 'green gaps' between villages. This decision was also appealed, and this time the Inspector agreed with the developer's argument that policy NE4 was a policy for the supply of housing and had to be considered out of date. The Council challenged that decision and in the High Court Lang J ruled that "The immediate context of paragraph 49 suggests that the Minister intended to refer to policies for the supply of housing rather than to any policy which may have the indirect effect of restricting housing development". She agreed with the Council that NE4 was not a housing policy, did not come within the scope of paragraph 49 of the Framework and that it was an "error of law" to say that it did. The original decision to refuse permission was reinstated.

When both parties appealed against the Supperstone/Lang judgments, the cases were conjoined and considered primarily by Lindblom LJ in a judgment was issued on 17 March 2016[11]. This identified the central question: should a 'narrow' or 'broad' interpretation of paragraph 49 be applied by decision makers. A narrow interpretation would limit the application of paragraph 49 to "policies dealing only with the numbers and distribution of new housing"; a wide one would include policies "whose effect is to restrain the supply by restricting housing development in certain

10 Cheshire East Borough Council v Secretary of State for Communities and Local Government & Anor [2015] EWHC 410 (Admin)

11 Suffolk Coastal District Council v Hopkins Homes Ltd & Anor [2016] EWCA Civ 168

parts of the authority's area". He ruled that a broader interpretative approach should be adopted, with Framework interpreted in the context of its primary goal of delivering more housing, stating that "Interpreting the policy in this way does not strain the natural and ordinary meaning of the words its draftsman has used. It does no violence at all to the language." He agreed with Supperstone J in that the Inspector had adopted too narrow a definition and overruled Lang J's judgement: "her interpretation of the policy was not correct…".

The judgment was highly significant. For local authorities without a five-year supply of housing land as required by paragraph 47, it meant that any policy that could – directly or indirectly – restrict housing developments would come within the scope of paragraph 49, automatically triggering a presumption in favour of sustainable development. Unsurprisingly the case was appealed to the Supreme Court who issued its judgment in May 2017[12].

Lord Carnwath began by noting that "Unaided by the legal arguments, I would have regarded the meaning of paragraph 49 itself, taken in context, as reasonably clear, and not susceptible to much legal analysis". He adopted the 'narrow' approach, ruling that it was wrong to "adopt a reading of paragraph 49 which not only changes its language, but in doing so creates a form of non-statutory fiction." He also stressed that the weight given to policies should be a "pure planning judgement, not dependent on issues of legal interpretation" and that there should be no "legalistic exercise" to decide whether policies were within paragraph 49. The case resolved the meaning of the six words it was asked to consider but it does not seem to have

---

12 Suffolk Coastal District Council v Hopkins Homes Ltd & Anor [2017] UKSC 37,

limited the role of lawyers as interpreters of policy – despite the introduction of a revised Framework.

The 2018 Framework and the 2019 Framework

On 24th July 2018 James Brokenshire, the Secretary of State for Housing, Communities and Local Government on 24th July 2018 introduced a new Framework as a "comprehensive approach to ensuring the right homes are built in the right places".[13] A fresh version of that Framework, with some minor changes, was published in 2019. The document retains the presumption in favour of sustainable development in Paragraph 11 but the wording is different. The 2019 Framework states that for decisions on individual applications the presumption in favour of sustainable development means:

- approving development proposals that accord with an up-to-date development plan without delay; or
- where there are no relevant development plan policies, or the policies which are most important for determining the application are out-of-date, granting permission unless:
    - the application of policies in this Framework that protect areas or assets of particular importance provides a clear reason for refusing the development proposed; or
    - any adverse impacts of doing so would significantly and demonstrably outweigh the benefits, when

13 https://hansard.parliament.uk/Commons/2018-07-24/debates/18072456000029/Housing

> assessed against the policies in this Framework taken as a whole."

The policies referred to as providing a 'clear reason' for refusal are defined in footnote 6 to the Framework as "relating to: habitats sites (and those sites ... Sites of Special Scientific Interest; land designated as Green Belt, Local Green Space, an Area of Outstanding Natural Beauty, a National Park (or within the Broads Authority) or defined as Heritage Coast; irreplaceable habitats; designated heritage assets... other heritage assets of archaeological interest... and areas at risk of flooding or coastal change."

The wording of the presumption has changed, but the evaluation of whether or not permission should be granted still requires decision makers to assess sustainable development in terms of its compliance with the Framework. It is therefore likely that the underlying issues of interpretation addressed in 'Suffolk Coastal' will persist. The *East Bergholt*[14] case – the first to consider the merits of a planning decision in the context of the new Framework – is perhaps just the first of these. Babergh District Council granted permission for a residential development in East Bergholt where in the absence of a 5-year housing land supply the paragraph 14 presumption applied. The local parish council asserted that in applying the Framework the council misinterpreted the word "deliverable" in footnote 11 of the 2012 Framework. By the time the case was considered the new Framework was in place with a fresh definition of "deliverable" in its glossary. The judge, confirming the Council's decision as correct, was asked to consider both definitions, but ruled simply that "Whether or not a site is deliverable, and whether there will be

14 East Bergholt Parish Council v Babergh District Council [2018] EWHC 3400 (Admin)

delivery, are matters of planning judgment". The fact that the challenge was brought on the basis of interpretation of one word in the Framework suggests that, despite *Hopkins Homes,* there is substantial scope for future arguments of the same kind.

CHAPTER TWO
MATERIAL CONSIDERATIONS

Having identified the relevant development plan policies and given them appropriate weight, the decision maker's attention needs to turn to the considerations material to that application and give appropriate weight to them. This process was also explained in detail in by Lord Clyde in the 1997 *City of Edinburgh*[1] case:

> "*He will also have to identify all the other material considerations which are relevant to the application and to which he should have regard. He will then have to note which of them support the application and which of them do not, and he will have to assess the weight to be given to all of these considerations. He will have to decide whether there are considerations of such weight as to indicate that the development plan should not be accorded the priority which the statute has given to it. And having weighed these considerations and determined these matters he will require to form his opinion on the disposal of the application.*"

Unlike the development plan there is no statutory definition of a material consideration. The *Stringer*[2] case did however establish the principle that "any consideration which relates to the use and development of land is capable of being a planning consideration". This means that the scope of material considerations is not only wide but will fluctuate depending on the particular proposal considered. This section will consider

---

1 City of Edinburgh Council v Secretary of State for Scotland 1998 SC (HL) 33,

2 Stringer v Minister of Housing and Local Governemnt [1971] 1 All E.R. 65

- Material considerations that are also regulated by separate legislative requirements;

- Material considerations where policy assigns a particular status to them and/or requires them to be applied in a certain way;

- Material considerations established through practice or case law

It will then consider specific factors that while not directly related to planning are essential elements of public decision making: the Public Sector Equality Duty '(PSED') and international rights established under the Human Rights Act ('HRA').

Considerations that are material as a matter of law

Section 70 of the 1990 itself establishes two considerations that are material as a matter of law: a post-examination draft neighbourhood plan where its policies are relevant to the consent in question; and any local finance considerations.

- The emerging neighbourhood plan must as a matter of law be taken into account as a material consideration where: i) the local authority has formally decided to carry out a referendum; or ii) the Secretary of State has directed that there should be a referendum; or iii) an examiner has recommended that a plan should be made with or without modification.

- Local finance considerations are also a material consideration as a matter of law. This does not apply to all financial considerations but only: i) grants or other financial assistant from the government; or ii) a sum or sums that have been, will be or could be received through the Community Infrastructure Levy.

In addition, there are a number of issues that are always material planning considerations under the legal test, but are also required to be taken into account in a specific way by a separate legislative requirement. These include considerations relating to a listed building, a conservation area and the environmental implications of proposals of a certain size or nature. Ignoring these duties or applying them in the wrong way, will be a legal defect in the decision-making process whether or not they are taken into account as material considerations.

Material Considerations with parallel legal duties:

<u>Environmental Impact Assessment ('EIA')</u>

The European Communities Act 1972 provides that EU law will prevail over 'any enactment passed or to be passed' by the United Kingdom Parliament.' European Directives give rights that can be asserted by individuals and that must be safeguarded by the courts. European environmental assessment processes in particular introduce and enforce rigorous empirical standards on the development consent process in England through Directives aimed at identifying, assessing and mitigating their environmental impacts.

The Environmental Impacts Assessment ('EIA') Directive was made in 1985.[3] Recital (2) states that "[pursuant] to Article 191 of the Treaty on the Functioning of the European Union, Union policy on the environment is based on the precautionary principle ...", and that "[effects] on the environment should be taken into account at the earliest possible stage ...". Article 3(1) requires assessment of "the direct and indirect significant effects of a project ...". Paragraph 5 of Annex IV states that "... [the] description of the likely significant effects on the factors specified in Article 3(1) should cover the direct effects and any indirect, secondary, cumulative, transboundary, short-term, medium-term and long-term, permanent and temporary, positive and negative effects of the project ...".

The current regulations were made in 2011[4] and the most recent version is the Town and Country Planning (Environmental Impact Assessment) Regulations 2017 ("the EIA regulations")[5]. These principles are enacted in the Regulation 2 requirement that in the determination of planning applications the environmental statement must be taken into account along with any representations made about likely environmental effects.

The scope of the duty has been considered many times in the courts, and it is beyond the scope of this book to cover the case law in detail. However, environmental and ecological issues play an increasingly significant role in planning decisions, especially in relation to air quality. Local authorities need to be very careful how environmental

---

3 Council Directive 85/337/EEC

4 Town and Country Planning (Environmental Impact Assessment) (England and Wales) Regulation 2011 (SI2011/1824)

5 The Town and Country Planning (Environmental Impact Assessment) Regulations 2017 (SI2017 / 571).

impacts are assessed and reported in the context of planning decisions, so it is worth being aware of two of the most recent and significant cases involving both issues.

The first is the Court of Appeal decision in January 2018 considering a proposal for 'fracking' in two sites in Lincolnshire[6]. The grounds of the challenge included the assertion that there was insufficient compliance with EIA requirements, in particular that the Inspector: failed to give enough weight to cumulative effects; should have given greater weight to potentially significant effects; discounted evidence of uncertainty over the possible effects of the development on human health; and should not have assumed that the existing regulatory regime would operate effectively. Lord Justice Lindblom dismissed these grounds, stating that:

- it was unnecessary and inappropriate to include environmental effects of unknown development in the EIA;
- the Secretary of State was entitled to regard the environmental statement as compliant with the definition in the EIA regulations;
- it was not the task of the court to review evidence relating to human health; and that
- there was no evidence to negate the policy principles that pollution control regimes would operate effectively.

6 Preston New Road Action Group v Secretary of State for Communities & Anor [2018] EWCA Civ 9

The next is another Court of Appeal judgment, issued in January this year, which considered whether it was lawful under the air quality regime (Directive 2008/50/EC and the Air Quality Standards Regulations 2010) for the Secretary of State not to call in an application for housing in Canterbury[7]. They asserted that the Secretary of State had erred in law when he failed to take into account his obligation to maintain threshold values of air quality when deciding not to call in the application. Lindblom J acknowledged in paragraph 48 of his judgment that "The likely effects of a proposed development on air quality are material considerations in the making of the decision on the application for planning permission, to be taken into account alongside other material considerations weighing for or against the proposal." However, he also ruled that:

- the preparation and implementation of an air quality plan complying with article 23 was the correct remedy under the Air Quality Directive: "Article 23 does not require any steps beyond the preparation and implementation of an efficacious air quality plan."

- The air quality regime did not constrain the Secretary of State's discretion so as to require the application to be decided by him "it does not have the effect of narrowing the Secretary of State's call-in discretion in such circumstances, let alone of transforming that discretion into a duty"

7 Shirley & Anor, R (On the Application Of) v Secretary of State for Housing, Communities and Local Government [2019] EWCA Civ 22

Birds and Habitats Directive

Directive 2009/147/EC – the Birds Directive establishes a European network of special Protection Areas to guard against habitat loss and degradation that could threaten the conservation of wild birds[8]. The 2010 regulations require the effect of granting a consent on such a site to be given considered before any such consent is granted. Directive 92/43/EEC – the Habitats Directive – also establishes a site networks where the land is recognised as ecologically valuable and is safeguarded against potentially damaging developments[9]. Article 6(3) of the Directive requires an appropriate assessment to be carried out where a plan or project is likely to have a significant effect on one of these European sites, whether individually or in combination with other projects. Article 6(4) states that where a negative assessment is recorded consent should not be granted except in specific limited circumstances.

Habitats assessments have become a hot topic recently because of two decisions in the European courts. In the 'People over Wind' case[10] consent was granted for a wind farm, and the company subsequently applied for consent to lay a cable connecting it to the electricity grid. Consents of this kind did not normally need planning permission, but did require screening for whether or not an appropriate assessment under the Habitats Directive was required.

The screening in this case decided that an appropriate assessment was not needed, but took into account mitigation measures when making

8 Directive 2009/147/EC

9 Council Directive 92/43/EEC

10 C-323/17 – People Over Wind and Sweetman

that decision. The High Court (Ireland) asked for a ruling from the Court of Justice of the European Union as to whether or not this was the correct approach. The Court ruled that it was not: "in order to determine whether it is necessary to carry out, subsequently, an appropriate assessment of the implications... of a plan or project it is not appropriate, at the screening stage, to take account of the measures intended to avoid or reduce the harmful effects of the plan or project on that site".

The consequences of this is that when a proposal is screened for its impacts on a habitats site, that screening process must not take mitigation into account. In addition, the Government subsequently amended paragraph 177 of the Framework so that where an appropriate assessment has been carried out and there are no adverse impacts on a habitats site, the presumption in favour of sustainable development can apply, where previously it was excluded.

The subsequent *Holohan*[11] case was another reference from the Irish High Court, challenging a decision to grant consent for the proposed Kilkenny Northern Ring Road Extension which would, if constructed, cross the River Nore Special Protection Area and River Barrow and River Nore Site of Community Importance. The CJEU ruled that an appropriate assessment must catalogue the entirety of habitat types and species, identify and examine the implications of the proposed project for the species on that site and – in some circumstances – outside it. It also ruled that reasons must be given for rejecting findings in an expert scientific opinion, and that the developer should supply information addressing the significant effects of the proposed project on all species identified in the envir-

11 Case C-461/17 *Holohan v. An Bord Pleanála*

onmental statement, and the impact of the same project on the alternative sites studied.

Waste Directives

Directive 2008/98 sets the basic concepts and definitions related to waste management and requires that waste be managed without endangering human health and harming the environment, and in particular without risk to water, air, soil, plants or animals, without causing a nuisance through noise or odours, and without adversely affecting the countryside or places of special interest. It is transposed into English law through the Waste Regulations[12]. Regulation 18 requires a planning authority to have regard to Article 13, and Article 16 (1), (2) and (3) when determining planning applications.

Listed Buildings and Conservation Areas

Section 66 of the Planning (Listed Buildings and Conservation Areas) Act 1990 requires that when considering whether to grant planning permission for development which affects a listed building or its setting the local authority must have "regard to the desirability of preserving the building or its setting or any features of special architectural or historic interest which it possesses." Similar considerations apply to conservation areas: where the development is within or adjacent to a conservation area sections 72 and 73 of the same Act requires that the decision must be taken including 'special regard' to the 'desirability of preserving or enhancing' the character or appearance of the area.[13]

---

12 Waste (England and Wales) Regulations 2011 SI 2011/988

13 Section 66(1) of the Planning (Listed Buildings and Conservation Areas) Act 1990

The 2014 *Forge Field*[14] decision established that "when an authority finds that a proposed development would harm the setting of a listed building or the character or appearance of a conservation area, it must give that harm considerable importance and weight" and this was confirmed in 2018 when Justice Kerr confirmed in the *Shimbles*[15] case that "the committee must not, in the context of harm to a heritage asset or its setting, merely carry out "a simple unweighted balancing exercise". In another case in 2018[16] Lord Justice Lindblom considered the meaning of 'the setting' of an asset and confirmed that it might be affected either by development within the setting of a listed building or outside the setting, though there had to be a distinct visual relationship between the two that should be more than remote or ephemeral. This year a proposal involving conversion of a historic house and grounds into 12 apartments[17] was quashed because it did not pay sufficient regard to the conservation team response, which had the effect of 'downplaying' their concerns in the planning balance.

Material considerations where policy prescribes treatment

For a number of planning considerations, they are not solely material considerations to be taken into account under the legal test but are also, under the Framework, required to be taken into account in a particular way by the decision maker.

---

14 (Forge Field Society) v. Sevenoaks DC [2014] EWHC 1895(Admin)

15 Shimbles, R (On the Application Of) v Bradford Metropolitan District Council [2018] EWHC 195 (Admin)

16 Catesby Estates Ltd v Peter Steer, Historic England and SSCLG [2018] EWCA Civ 1697

17 Liverpool Open And Green Spaces Community Interest Company, R (On the Application Of) v Liverpool City Council [2019] EWHC 55 (Admin)

Paragraph 11 of the Framework provides that where the presumption in favour of sustainable development is applied permission should be granted "unless the application of policies in this Framework that protect areas or assets of particular importance provides a clear reason for refusing the development proposed." These policies are listed in the footnote to paragraph 11 as follows "habitats sites (and those sites listed in paragraph 176) and/or designated as Sites of Special Scientific Interest; land designated as Green Belt, Local Green Space, an Area of Outstanding Natural Beauty, a National Park (or within the Broads Authority) or defined as Heritage Coast; irreplaceable habitats; designated heritage assets (and other heritage assets of archaeological interest referred to in footnote 63); and areas at risk of flooding or coastal change."

Because these policies determine whether or not the presumption is applied, it is essential that they are taken into account exactly in the way the Framework requires. When dealing with sites that come within any of these categories, it is a good idea to refer to the Framework and what it requires the decision-maker to do when taking them into consideration, in order to avoid allegations that there has been misinterpretation or misapplication of the Framework in the decision-making process.

Habitats sites This does not just refer to sites regulated by the Habitats Regulations considered above: paragraph 176 of the Framework is clear that the reference to 'Habitats sites' in this context includes potential Special Protection Areas, possible Special Areas of Conservation, listed or proposed Ramsar sites and sites identified for compensatory measures for adverse effects on any of them. In addition, the Framework Glossary has another definition of Habitats sites which includes Sites of Community Importance and Marine

Sites. When land comes within any of these designations, the paragraph 11 presumption will not apply unless an appropriate assessment has concluded that the plan or project will not adversely affect its integrity.

Sites designated as Sites of Special Scientific Interest: These are defined in the Glossary as Sites designated by Natural England under the Wildlife and Countryside Act 1981 and paragraph 175 of the Framework provides that development should not normally be permitted on them unless the benefits 'clearly outway' its immediate and broader impact.

Green Belt: Protecting Green Belt land has its own section in the Framework and a number of criteria that need to be applied in the decision-making process. The fundamental principle is in paragraph 143 – that inappropriate development should not be approved except in very special circumstances. All new buildings are considered inappropriate – including 'many renewable energy projects' unless they come within the 5 exceptions listed in paragraph 145 and a further limited range of developments is listed in paragraph 146. All other developments will have to show that 'very special circumstances' apply and these are not defined except in the case of renewable energy projects where the wider environmental benefits may amount to justification.

Local Green Space: This is a relatively new type of designation of land and generally occurs as part of the adoption or revision of a neighbourhood plan. Paragraph 100 of the Framework sets out a number of criteria to be taken into account when considering whether or not a Local Green Space should be designated and also states that policies for its management should be consistent with those for Green Belts. Local Green Spaces have been the subject of two cases, which demonstrate how controversial and significant the designation can be. In *Legard*[18] the proposed designation of Local Green Space in the St Quintin and Woodlands Neighbourhood Plan was challenged, primarily on the basis of the way that the Council had managed the process, but also considered the designation itself and the way in which the relevant paragraph (then paragraph 77 of the Framework) should be applied. More recently in a case involving Udney Park Playing Fields in Richmond[19] a local plan was successfully challenged when the effect of the Inspector's recommendations on the designation was not properly reflected in the following consultation.

Landscape designations: This applies to Areas of Outstanding Natural Beauty (AONB), National Parks, Heritage Coast or land within a Broads Authority and is considered in section 15 of the Framework which states that weight must be given to the need to preserve conserve and enhance landscape, scenic beauty, wildlife and cultural heritage. It also establishes the principle that permission should be refused for major developments on land in these areas except in exceptional circumstances where it can be demonstrated that the proposal is in the public interest.

Irreplaceable habitats: Unlike Green Belt or AONB this is not a term with a widely accepted or established definition, they are referred to only in paragraph 175 of the Framework, and this gives just examples: ancient woodland and ancient or veteran trees. The

18 Legard, R (On the Application Of) v The Royal Borough of Kensington and Chelsea [2018] EWHC 32 (Admin)

19 Jopling v Richmond-Upon-Thames London Borough Council & Anor [2019] EWHC 190 (Admin)

Framework does go on to say that planning permission should be refused when it leads to the loss or deterioration of these habitats, unless there are "wholly exceptional reasons"(footnote 58 states that this can include nationally significant infrastructure projects, orders under the Transport and Works Act and hybrid bills) or where the loss is outweighed by the public benefit and a suitable compensation strategy exists;

Designated heritage assets: As well as the separate statutory test to be applied to proposals involving listed buildings and conservation areas, section 16 of the Framework requires specific attention to be given to this wider class of land and buildings with recognised historic value. The class includes World Heritage Sites, Scheduled Monuments, Listed Buildings, Protected Wreck Sites, Registered Park and Gardens, Registered Battlefields and Conservation Areas. Footnote 63 to paragraph 194 also includes within this definition "non-designated heritage assets of archaeological interest, which are demonstrably of equivalent significance to scheduled monuments". It requires weight to be given to the conservation of the asset and 'clear and convincing' justification to be supplied for any harm to or loss of the asset. It directs that permission should be refused for such proposals except in limited – and defined – circumstances, though it allows the public benefits of such a proposal to be taken into account in the interests of securing an optimum viable use.

Areas at risk of flooding or coastal change: This is primarily dealt with in section 14 of the Framework. The primary recommendation is that inappropriate development (a term undefined in this context) should be avoided in areas at risk of flooding and that if such risk is necessary the development should not increase flood risk 'elsewhere' (another undefined term). Paragraph 158 then states that a sequential test should be applied in areas known to be at risk "now or in the future from any form of flooding" but that it may not need to be applied if such a test informed the land designation in the plan, and an exception test, contained in paragraph 160, may be applied where lower risk sites are unavailable. Paragraph 163 then sets out the criteria that need to be applied for proposals in areas at risk of flooding, paragraph 164 confirms that these should be applied for some minor development and changes of use. Finally, paragraph 165 recommends specific sustainable drainage systems to be included in all proposals for major development.

Material considerations established through practice or case law

As stated above, there is no legal definition of material considerations. However, there are a range of matters that are accepted, through practice and common law, to be material to most if not all planning decisions.

National Policy

This will always include the Framework, online guidance such as the National Planning Policy Guidance ('NPPG') and Written Ministerial Statements ('WMS'). The decision maker does not have to adhere to the policy as if it were law, but where there is a departure from it clear and sound reasons should be given. This was confirmed recently in a challenge raised by Friends of the Earth[20] to its validity generally, where Justice Dove confirmed in paragraph 29 of his judgment that "it is beyond argument that the Framework is such a material consideration to be taken into account." The NPPG has

20 Friends of the Earth Ltd v Secretary of State for Housing, Communities And Local Government [2019] EWHC 518 (Admin)

also been recently examined by the courts[21] where in a case involving a retail development in Bideford it was asserted that the NPPG was not applied correctly. The judge in this case did not question the materiality of the NPPG but did urge caution in its application. She noted that it was not subject to consultation, not drafted "by or for lawyers" and must be considered as guidance not policy and not "interpreted and applied in an overly legalistic way" This case establishes that the way in which the NPPG is taken into account is a matter of planning judgment for the local authority – but even so, it should not be ignored.

Like the NPPG, Written Ministerial Statements are not subject to consultation or external scrutiny before they are issued. Unlike the NPPG they can have an immediate and considerable impact on the way in which planning permissions are determined. For example, on 28 November 2014 the Secretary of State for Communities and Local Government issued a WMS which among other things excluded developments of 10 units or less from affordable housing contributions. This meant that any development plan or other policies containing such statements were immediately out of date and could not be applied. The legitimacy of the statement was questioned by West Berkshire and the Court of Appeal gave the final ruling on the matter in May 2016.[22] The ruling confirmed that such a statement made in parliament would not only be a material consideration to all relevant planning decisions but could also have the effect of overriding specific development plan policies in local authority plans. Written Ministerial Statements can therefore make significant changes to planning policy without needing to be con-

21 Solo Retail Limited v Torridge District Council [2019] EWHC 489 (Admin)

22 Secretary of State for Communities and Local Government v West Berkshire District Council & Anor [2016] EWCA Civ 441

sulted on first and without a great amount of justification and must be given appropriate attention and weight in decisions where they are relevant.

Emerging Plans: Emerging plans – including emerging neighbourhood plans – are also relevant as material considerations, a principle recognised in both national guidance and case law. In a recent consideration of the issue in the Courts is a case involving Stratford on Avon District Council[23] Mr Justice Hickinbottom noted that plans are often under review and alteration and ruled that "where a plan is going through the rigorous and often lengthy process I have described, that emerging plan is also a material consideration." Paragraph 48 of the Framework confirms both that weight may be given and the factors to be taken into account when deciding how much weight to give, but paragraph 49 qualifies the extent to which such an emerging plan can constitute a reason for refusal.

Previous Decisions: Planning appeal decisions are not binding in the same way that a court judgment would be but they are a material consideration in a planning decision – a principle established in *North Wiltshire*[24] The weight of previous decisions has recently been considered by the Court of Appeal in relation to a decision of the Secretary of State[25] where an appeal decision was quashed because it was irreconcilable to another recent decision on similar facts. The Court confirmed that previous decisions were capable of being material considerations. It also advised that the Secretary of State was

23 Stratford On Avon District Council v Secretary of State for Communities and Local Government [2013] EWHC 2074

24 North Wiltshire DC v Secretary of State for the Environment (1993) 65 P & CR 137

25 DLA Delivery Ltd v Baroness Cumberlege of Newick & Anor (Rev 1) [2018] EWCA Civ 1305

obliged to take "reasonable steps" to ensure that his decisions were consistent with his own decisions on cases of the same kind. It is sensible to apply this advice to local authority decisions too.

Representations from the community: Representations made by the public are always material considerations – and indeed must be taken into account when they are submitted in response to a consultation on a planning application. Although the impact on an individual may be a material consideration, issues such as impact on the amenity of the community as a whole, or traffic impacts on an area generally, will generally be given more weight than the impact on private interests such as loss of a view, or impact on a business, or overlooking.

Matters regulated by other statutory codes: Issues can still be material even if they are regulated by separate legislation. This can be relevant to matters such as health and safety, licensing, and building control, and is increasingly problematic when it comes to issues such as air quality and other environmental impacts. All of these factors are capable of being considered material considerations and should not be excluded from the scope of the decision-makers discretion simply because they are separately regulated. However, the weight given by the local authority should be informed by the content of that legislation to avoid overlapping or inconsistent approaches.

Section 106 Agreements: Planning obligations are public benefits secured under section 106 of the 1990 Act through legal agreements connected to and dependent on the issue of the relevant permission. They are intended to mitigate the impacts of a development proposal, or 'outweigh' its disbenefits. They can be used to prescribe the nature of development (for example, requiring a given portion of housing is affordable); compensate for loss or damage created by a development (for example, loss of open space); mitigate a development's impact (for example, through increased public transport provision) through works, restrictions on the proposed development or the payment of money.

Regulation 2010 of the 2010 Community Infrastructure Regulations[26] imposed a new legal test on 106 obligations, so that a planning obligation could only be relied on as a reason for granting planning permission where it was (a) necessary to make the development acceptable in planning terms; (b)directly related to the development; and (c) fairly and reasonably related in scale and kind to the development. In 2012 one judge said that "There is nothing novel in regulation 122 except the fact that it is contained in a statutory instrument."[27] However, in 2016 a different judge acknowledged that "there are now tests in law which to some degree were not tests of law before their enactment". [28]

In 2018 the *H J Banks*[29] case raised the issue of whether an obligation could be taken into account as "material" to a planning decision even where it was not strictly "necessary" within the requirements of regulation 122. Ouseley J considered a challenge to a refusal on appeal for a surface mine. The Inspector had divided the obligations into those which did comply with the requirement in

26 Community Infrastructure Regulations 2010 SI 2010/948

27 R (Welcome Break Group Limited) v Stroud District Council [2012] EWHC 140 (Admin)

28 Working Title Films Ltd, R (on the application of) v Westminster City Council & Anor [2016] EWHC 1855 (Admin)

29 HJ Banks & Company Ltd v Secretary of State for Housing Communities And Local Government [2018] EWHC 3141

regulation 122 and those which did not, and gave 'moderate weight' to the second category as general planning benefits though they were not relied on as reasons for the grant of permission. Ouseley considered whether these obligations which were not CIL compliant could still be a material considerations. He ruled that a planning obligation could be given weight in the planning balance even if it was not CIL compliant and that it was not unreasonable to distinguish between obligations that were among the reasons for the grant of permission and those that were just material considerations.

Social Objectives: The 2012 Copeland[30] case established that planning decisions can take into account a wide range of other social objectives. This case considered whether a policy document that aimed to restrict fast food outlets being approved near schools could legitimately be taken into account as a material consideration and confirmed that where youth obesity was a genuine social concern such documents could be taken into account. Since then obesity – particularly among children – has become more of an issue and is certainly capable of being considered as a legitimate planning considerations.

Other Matters: Other matters routinely considered to be material considerations are: the planning history of the site, the risk of creating a precedent for a particular kind of development or use in a specific area; the 'fallback position' of the use or development that could occur if permission were refused; concerns about public safety, and the availability of alternative sites for the same use or development. Local policies contained in documents other than the development plan_are also material considerations. The weight to be

30 R (Copeland) v London Borough of Tower Hamlets 2011

given to them will depend on a number of factors including relevance to the development as a whole, how widely the policy was consulted, how recently the policy was adopted and the extent to which it is consistent with the superior policy context.

Human Rights and the Public Sector Equality Duty ("PSED")

As well as considerations that are material in planning terms, there are overarching considerations that must be taken into account by all public authorities when making decisions. The Human Rights Act 1998 is the source of a number of human rights that can be asserted and enforced in the context of such decisions and the elements most relevant to planning are Article 1 of the First Protocol (the protection of property) and Article 8 (the right to respect for private and family life) The cases of South Bucks District Council v Porter (1) and (2) in 2003 and 2004 respectively established that where a local authority was seeking an injunction to remove travellers from land, personal circumstances relevant to these rights must be taken into account or the decisions would be invalidated and cases since including *Buckley*[31] *Varey*[32] and *Chapman*[33] have confirmed that position. The *Stevens*[34] case has additionally established that where family members include children, article 8 rights have to be interpreted in the light of general principles of international law, including those deriving from article 3(1) of the UN Convention on the Rights of the Child.

---

31 Buckley v United Kingdom app no 20348/92 [1996] ECHR 39

32 Varey v United Kingdom app no 26662/95 [2000] ECHR 692

33 Chapman v United Kingdom app no 27238/95 [2001] ECHR 43

34 Stevens v Secretary of State for Communities and Local Government & Anor [2013] EWHC 792 (Admin)

The most recent consideration of this issue in planning is a case involving the Environment Agency[35]. The owners of a farm adjacent to the River Severn claimed that the Environment Agency adopted a strategy for flood protection without properly assessing the burden imposed and breached Article 1 of the First Protocol and Article 14 of the Convention – the right to freedom from discrimination. The claim was dismissed on the basis that: the policies were "based on expert assessments; the Environment Agency was "even-handed in its approach to works" and there was no evidence that the works would create more of a flood risk. The policy did involve interference with land but it was "evident that there has been a fair balancing of their rights with those of the general interest as required by if these are to occur lawfully" In addition the article 14 rights were not engaged because "the claimed discrimination was not on the basis of a personal characteristic" and in any case there was "enough of a relevant difference to justify the different treatment".

The Public Sector Equality Duty or 'PSED' was introduced by section 149 of the 2010 Equality Act, and requires public bodies to have due regard to the needs of members of the population who have a protected status when exercising any public function. Its relevance to planning case was established in *Harris*[36] and explored and confirmed in *Coleman*[37] where claims established that a lack of proper regard to the particular needs of specific communities in the determination of planning applications, resulted in a breach of the Equality Act and led to the permissions being quashed.

35 King & Ors v Environment Agency [2018] EWHC 65 (QB)

36 Harris, R (on the application of) v The London Borough of Haringey [2010] EWCA Civ 703

37 Coleman, R (on the application of) v The London Borough of Barnet Council & Ors [2012] EWHC 3725

The most recent consideration, in a property context, of the application of the PSED is the *Peters* case.[38] This was a challenge to the decision of Haringay Council to create the Haringey Development Vehicle in partnership with a private sector developer, and is particularly relevant in a time when local authorities are seeking innovative ways to deliver their functions while saving money. One of the grounds of the challenge was that the Council failed to apply the public section equality duty. Mr Justice Ouseley rejected the challenge: "In my judgment, the Council was entitled to structure its decision-making in the way it did…It considered the equalities impact of the means whereby it chose to pursue its strategic objective. He also noted that "the s149 duty is not a duty to produce EqIAs. It is to have "due regard" to the issues." This is a timely reminder that it is the essence of the way in which the impacts are taken into account, and not the comprehensiveness of the form filling, that will be tested by the courts.

The PSED has also recently been successfully asserted in the context of a planning application.[39] The first involved an application for outline permission to redevelop part of an estate involving the demolition of up to 542 dwellings and the provision of up to 700 dwellings. The challenge asserted that the Council had failed to have "due regard" to the impact of its decision on members of the community who had the characteristics age, disability, race and pregnancy or maternity. The challenge was successful with Justice Lewis confirming that the duty applied to outline as well as full consents; that the central issue was "the impact on the elderly and the disabled of losing their existing homes that insufficient regard had

38 Peters v London Borough of Haringey & Anor [2018] EWHC 192 (Admin)

39 Buckley, R (on the application of) v Bath and North East Somerset Council & Anor [2018] EWHC 1551 (Admin)

been paid to it: "I am persuaded there were matters relevant to the discharge of the public sector equality duty which the relevant decision-maker needed to have due regard to but which were not drawn to the decision-maker's attention"

Conclusion

The importance of identifying all of the material considerations cannot be underestimated – as Lord Clyde noted in the *City of Edinburgh* decision, if the decision maker "fails to take account of some material consideration or takes account of some consideration which is irrelevant to the application his decision will be open to challenge." Decisions taken without any regard to a material consideration will be invalid. Similarly, decisions taken where weight has been place on an immaterial consideration will be equally vulnerable to a successful challenge. However, Lord Clyde went on to say that "the assessment of the considerations can only be challenged on the ground that it is irrational or perverse." This confirmed the principle established in an earlier House of Lords ruling on a 1995 case[40] that confirmed that a particular factor could be a material consideration, if it had "some connection with the proposed development which is not de minimis" but that "the extent, if any, to which it should affect the decision is a matter entirely within the discretion of the decision maker.

The courts have consistently defended the scope of this discretionary function and show no appetite to interfere in legal challenges where those challenges are concerned primarily with the application rather than the interpretation of policy. The court will interpret policies

40 Tesco Stores Ltd v Secretary of State for the Environment & Ors [1995] UKHL 22

"objectively in accordance with the language used, read as always in its proper context" - principles established by the Supreme Court in 2012 and confirmed in *Hopkins Homes.* However the courts recognise that a plans and policies will not be interpreted as if they were statutes or contracts, and the exercise of the local authorities judgment in applying the policies "can only be challenged on the ground that it is irrational or perverse".

For anyone faced with making a planning decision, this is comforting reading. It is important to identify the plan, to give it its proper weight, to identify all potentially material considerations and to take them into account, and to ensure that sufficient regard is paid to human rights and/or equality issues. But once this is done, the actual decision is still for the planning judgment of the officer or committee taking it – and the courts will only interfere with the exercise of this judgment in specific, and restrictive, circumstances.

CHAPTER THREE
GOVERNANCE

This chapter looks at the legal and governance context of planning decisions. It begins with a short explanation of how all local authority decisions are made, how planning committees are established and regulated and the law relating to the delegation of decision making to officers. It goes on to look at the mechanics of the committee process including issues such as access to information and member conduct and interests including the interrelationship between bias and predetermination.

General Governance Context of Planning Decisions

The planning system is defined by acts of Parliament, legislation, case law, government policy and guidance dating back to the 1940s and a wide range of related legal, policy and governance considerations are involved in the planning process. Local authorities are created by Parliament as statutory corporations, and operate as single legal entities. They are given a number of functions, including the function under section 38(6) of the Planning and Compulsory Purchase Act 2004 and section 70(2) of the Town and Country Planning Act 1990, to determine planning applications – referred to in case law as the 'statutory scheme'. General powers relevant to the determination of planning applications are also contained in the Local Government Act 1972, and the Localism Act 2011.

A council must adopt a constitution, available for viewing by the public, setting out its governance, decision-making structure, standing orders and other rules and protocols[1]. There are three basic models of governance for local authorities:

- the Committee System, whereby the Council comprising all councillors appoints select committees of councillors and delegates functions to those committees and to officers.

- Executive Leader and Cabinet Model, where the Council continues to discharge 'non-executive functions', but there is a separate direct election of an Executive Mayor who then appoints a Cabinet of councillors and arranges for the discharge of the 'executive functions'

The Local Government Act 2000 established new political management structures for local authorities, separating functions between decision-making and scrutiny of those decisions. Part II of the Local Government Act 2000 provides for the discharge of a local authority's functions by an executive of the authority. Some planning decisions come within these 'executive' arrangements including the approval of the local plan and other planning policy documents. However, the Local Authorities (Functions and Responsibilities) Regulations 2000[2] specify functions that are not to be the responsibility of an authority's executive or are to be the responsibility of such an executive only to a limited extent or only in specified circumstances. Regulation 2(1) of these Regulations provides that the functions listed in Schedule 1 ("Schedule 1 functions") are not to be the responsibility of an authority's executive.

1 Part 1A Section 9P Local Government Act 2000

2 SI 2000/2853

Schedule 1 includes a range of planning decision functions including the determination of planning applications.

The Secretary of State has the power to take the decision-making power on a planning application out of the hands of the local planning authority through a process known as 'call in' under section 77 of the 1990 Act. It is a wide, but discretionary power and only a small number of applications are called in – it is the exception rather than the rule and the Government has recently confirmed that no reasons have to be given either way.[3]

Planning decisions are made, and decision notices are issued, in the name of the local authority –comprising all of the elected members for that body. The determination of applications is an administrative act and there is no general obligation to give a hearing but there is a common law duty of fairness, which means that decisions should be made after hearing from both or all the parties involved. In practice, this duty is fulfilled by delegating the general authority of a local authority to make planning decisions to a dedicated committee or sub-committee of elected members – and also to planning officers. The planning committee generally makes that decision on the basis of information provided by case officers in the form of a report which will usually also includes a recommendation as to how the application should be dealt with.

The determination of planning decisions is a regulatory and not an executive function. Therefore, most of the law relating to the establishment of planning committees is contained in the Local Government Act 1972. Section 101 (1) (a) allows a local authority to

3 https://www.parliament.uk/business/publications/written-questions-answers-statements/written-statement/Commons/2019-03-26/HCWS1452/

arrange for any of its functions to be carried out by a committee, a sub-committee or an officer of that authority (but not to a single member) and section 101 (12) specifically includes within that delegation "anything which is calculated to facilitate, or is conducive or incidental to, the discharge of any of those functions.". In *Friends of Hethell*[4] Sullivan LJ recognised that delegation arrangements made under section 101 could include conditions or limitations as to the extent of the delegation. Section 101(5) allows local authorities to exercise the decision-making function jointly. Section 102 deals with the mechanics of the appointment of committees. The membership and terms of office is set by the Council who may establish its own criteria for appointments and can revoke the authority of the committee or a single member of it. That power to revoke membership may not be delegated and must be exercised by the Council as a whole. No member is obliged to serve on a committee and can resign at any time.

In addition, it is essential that all committees reflect the political balance of the Council as a whole and this is secured through sections 15-17 of the Local Government and Housing Act 1989. The cumulative effect of the sections is to require proportionality across the formal activities of the authority, representing its overall political composition. This duty does not however extend to independent members. Section 15 imposes a legal duty on the local authority after an election to review the representation of different political groups in committees and ensure that allocations of membership of committees reflects the political balance of the local authority as a whole, section 16 imposes a legal duty to give effect to those allocations as

4 Friends of Hethel Ltd, R (on the application of) v South Norfolk District Council & Anor [2010] EWCA Civ 894 (30 July 2010) URL: *http://www.bailii.org/ew/cases/EWCA/Civ/2010/894.html*

soon as practicably possible and section 17 allows different arrangements to be put in place if there is vote to do this and no member votes against it

Section 100(G) of the Local Government Act 1972 requires all Councils to maintain a list of each member of its Council and the name and address of every member of each committee and sub-committee.

Decisions made by Officers

Planning committee decisions attract most attention, but the reality of planning practice is that most decisions are taken under delegated powers. It is also quite normal for a committee report to include delegation of specific aspects of future work to an officer – most commonly the terms of a section 106 agreement. Section 101 of the Local Government Act 1972 enables a Council to delegate powers directly to officers and the detailed scheme of delegation should be contained within the constitution of the council.

In *Cheshire County Counvil v Secretary of State*[5] it was established that the authority of an assistant solicitor to issue an enforcement notice was effective even when the powers referred to other officers and no specific enforcement power was given to the subordinate officer. *Carlton-Conway*[6] examined whether a planning officer was within the scope of the powers delegated to in the grant of a permission. Pill LJ ruled that "It is important that a planning officer purporting to exercise delegated powers should give careful and genuine consider-

---

5 Cheshire County Council v Secretary of State for the Environment [1988] JPL 30

6 Carlton-Conway, R (On the Application Of) v London Borough of Harrow [2002] EWCA Civ 927 (14 June 2002) URL: *http://www.bailii.org/ew/cases/EWCA/Civ/2002/927.html*

ation to the question whether the particular application with which he is concerned comes within the delegation." In this case the power was granted only in relation to cases where there was clarity on the facts and the policies. This was a complex case which clearly did not come within the scope of the power granted and so "The only rational decision would have been to refer the application to the committee to make the appropriate planning judgments".

In *Kides*[7] there was a gap of almost 5 years between the Committee resolution and the decision notice being issued and there had been changes in national policy during that time. Parker LJ ruled that where there was a new material consideration the officer could only issue a decision notice if he was satisfied that the council was aware of it, that the application was reconsidered with the new factor in mind and that on reconsideration the council " *would* reach (not *might* reach) the same decision." In *Pemberton International*[8] Lewis J confirmed that a scheme of delegation would be compatible with section 101 so long as it either identified the officers, or sets out the process by which the officers authorised to exercise certain functions. In this case the scheme authorised a group of officers to exercise a function and not a "freestanding" power of general further delegation.

Couves[9] involved a committee decision that resolved to grant planning permission subject to a section 106 agreement, with the

7 Kides, R (on the application of) v South Cambridgeshire District Council & Ors [2002] EWCA Civ 1370 (9 October 2002) URL: *http://www.bailii.org/ew/cases/EWCA/Civ/2002/1370.html*

8 Pemberton International Ltd v London Borough of Lambeth & Anor [2014] EWHC 1998 (Admin) (18 June 2014) URL: *http://www.bailii.org/ew/cases/EWHC/Admin/2014/1998.html*

9 Couves, R (On the Application Of) v Edinburgh House Estates Ltd [2015] EWHC 504 (Admin)

agreement to be negotiated by the planning officer. The planning permission was challenged on the basis that the officer did not have power to grant permission without an express delegation of that function, and/or had gone beyond such powers as were delegated. Mr Justice Ouseley reviewed the constitution for the way in which delegated powers were expressed. He noted that "the delegation structure, in the light of the submissions, is less transparent and clear than the Constitution promised" and that "There are parts of the structure and resolution which are open to doubt, and can be picked over by lawyers." but nevertheless concluded that it was commonplace for such powers to be delegated to an officer. While recognising that the resolution did not grant express power to negotiate the terms of the s106 agreement it "should not be searched for language giving delegated power to the officer, but rather for language removing the power."

Although the scope of delegated powers is broad and seems to be interpreted in a relatively relaxed way, these decisions may still be invalidated if they fail to take account of the Openness of Local Government Bodies Regulations 2014 [10] Regulation 7 requires a written record to be made of any decision delegated to an officer that would otherwise have been taken by the local authority, or a committee, sub-committee of and that either affect the rights of an individual; or awards a contract or incur expenditure which, in either case, materially affects that relevant local government body's financial position. This covers, although it is not limited to, planning decisions taken by officers and there is some relevant case law on this area:

10 http://www.legislation.gov.uk/uksi/2014/2095/contents/made

- In a case involving Maldon District Council[11] Howell J confirmed that where the decision on an application for the approval of "reserved matters" or of other matters requiring their approval under a condition is taken by the authority themselves or by one of their committees or sub-committees, there is no statutory requirement for reasons to be given for the decision. However, the 2014 Regulations require an officer to make a written record of certain decisions taken, "along with reasons for the decision" and "details of alternative options, if any considered and rejected", and thereafter to make that record and any background papers available for inspection on the authority's website and its office, in each case as soon as reasonably practicable: see regulations 6 to 8 of the 2014 Regulations. In this case all the officer did was endorse the recommendation the report contained, and "failed to exercise the discretion delegated" because she was "not in a position to do so". The decision was quashed.

- In the *Newey* case[12] failure to record a decision to approve a construction management plan submitted in satisfaction of a condition attracted the same criticism "there was here an obligation pursuant to Regulation 7 to provide a written record of the Decision. There was no written record here and accordingly the Council were in breach of its obligations under the regulations." This was also quashed.

In some circumstances, even where an officer has acted outside his or her authority the matter can be subsequently ratified, but not if an

11 Pearl, R (on the application of) v Maldon District Council & Anor [2018[EWHC 212 (Admin)

12 Newey, R (On the Application Of) v South Hams District Council [2018] EWHC 1872 (Admin)

individual's legal rights have already been affected – for example, where action has already been taken in relation to the grant of a permission or the issue of an enforcement notice. In addition, where an officer is acting within his or her apparent authority, the council may be bound by that action.

Committee Meetings

The principal legislative authority for committee meetings is the Local Government Act 1972, as amended by the Local Government (Access to Information) Act 1985 specifically section 100A. Much of the mechanics of committee meetings will be contained within the standing orders of the Council in question but these standing orders may not change or restrict the common law duties and rights of individual councillors. The provisions of s100A are extended to sub committees including planning sub committees by section 100E. Section 100A grants a general right of access to the meetings themselves, access to information relating to those meetings and sets out the requirements for giving notice of meetings. Section 100A(6) additionally requires the press to be given "reasonable facilities" for reporting on the meeting – with reporting including filming, photographing or making audio recordings under subsections 7A-7F. The general right of access is qualified by section 100A (3) which allows exclusion of the public where 'confidential information would be disclosed' and section 100A(4) which also allows exclusion of public and press when exempt information is to be discussed. Categories of exempt information are detailed in Schedule 12A to the 1972 Act – including specific qualifications. Section 100A (8) preserves a general power of exclusion to prevent "disorderly conduct or other misbehaviour'.

In terms of access to information this is primarily granted through section 100B. This requires 5 clear days advance notice of any meeting – excluding both the day of the meeting and the day on which notice is given. It also requires that agendas and reports should be available to members of the public for give clear days before the meeting though where information is 'exempt' it can be excluded (section 100B(2)). It is not uncommon for planning committees to have items added much less than five days before the meeting and although the section also includes provision for shorter time periods in some circumstances, the later items are added agenda the greater the risk of a challenge. In such circumstances the key issue is to ensure that the public are given access at the same time as members of the committee themselves.

Section 100C requires that a copy of the agenda, a copy of all reports and the minutes of the meeting must be made available for inspection for six years after the date of the meeting. The standard for the content and form of minutes was considered in 2018 in *Steer v Shepway*[13] in a case involving an application for a holiday park. Lang J applied the standards for reasons in planning decisions that were established in established in *South Buckinghamshire District Council v Porter*[14]: The reasons for a decision must be intelligible and they must be adequate. They must enable the reader to understand why the matter was decided as it was and what conclusions were reached on the "principal important controversial issues", disclosing how any issue of law or fact was resolved. Lang J noted that the absence of any reference to the criteria for the application of paragraph 116 of the NPPF, in particular, whether or not the proposed

---

13 Steer, R (On the Application Of) v Shepway District Council [2018] EWHC 238 (Admin)

14 [2004] 1 WLR 1953

development was a "major development", raised a real doubt as to whether the members did give proper consideration as to whether it applied, and if so, to what effect. In addition, she criticised the minutes because they did not explain why members concluded that there was no harm when the objectors (some of whom had specialist expertise) identified wide-ranging harm and even the supporting reports identified some harm. On balance she concluded that the minutes failed to meet the requirements established in because they did not "enable the reader to understand why the matter was decided as it was and what conclusions were reached on the 'principal important controversial issues', disclosing how any issue of law or fact was resolved"

Section 100H additionally requires that the documents should be open for inspection "at all reasonable hours" and states that copies may be taken of them, and also creates an offence where access is denied intentionally. Section 100D deals with background papers and requires that they too must be listed and available for inspection for four years. It is all too easy to forget about this requirement. In one case involving Northumberland County Council[15] a noise assessment was one of the essential documents relevant to a decision to grant planning permission for a wind turbine. However, there were no background papers listed in the report, and the report itself was uploaded to the Council's website only on the day before the meeting. Cranston J noted that "there were a number of breaches of the public's right to know under the Local Government Act 1972." He ruled that the noise assessment report came within the definition of background papers but was not listed in the report or made

---

15 Joicey, R (on the Application of) v Northumberland County Council [2014] EWHC 3657 (Admin) (07 November 2014) URL: *http://www.bailii.org/ew/cases/EWHC/Admin/2014/3657.html* Cite as: [2014] EWHC 3657 (Admin), [2015] PTSR 622

available either as part of the planning file or the committee papers – and that this was "a serious breach by the Council of its statutory obligations" and the permission was quashed.

Section 100F sets out rights of access to information about committee items that are specific to the elected members of the council and additional to any other rights they may have. They are based on the common law principle that a member of a council has a right to inspect documents 'addressed' to that council. However, the right does not extend to exempt information and must be justified on the basis that access is necessary to facilitate carrying out duties as a member of that particular committee – it is essential for the member who wants access to show that he or she has a "need to know" the information[16].

Member interests, Predetermination and Bias

<u>Member Interests</u>

Part Three of the Local Government Act 2000 established a new ethical framework for local government including the introduction of statutory codes of conduct. This was amended by the Localism Act 2011 which made fundamental changes to the system of regulation of standards of conduct for elected and co-opted councillors in England from 1 July 2012.

Chapter 7 of Part 1 of the Localism Act 2011 makes provision for the standards of conduct expected of members and co-opted members of relevant authorities in England. 'Relevant authorities'

---

16 R v Birmingham City Council Ex parte O. AND ANOTHER - [1982] 1 WLR 679

includes district, unitary, metropolitan, county authorities or London borough council, parish and town councils, fire and rescue authorities, transport or other joint authorities, National Parks, the GLA and the London Fire and Emergency Planning Authority.

Local authorities remain under a statutory duty to promote and maintain high standards of conduct for their elected and co-opted members and must adopt a new Code of Conduct governing elected and co-opted members' conduct when acting in that capacity. The new Code of Conduct must when viewed as a whole be consistent with the Nolan Committee's seven principles of public life: self-lessness integrity objectivity accountability, openness, honesty and leadership. The authority has a discretion as to what it includes within its new Code of Conduct, provided that it is consistent with these seven principles. The authority's Code of Conduct must also contain appropriate requirements for the registration (and disclosure) of pecuniary interests and non-pecuniary interests.

The Relevant Authorities (Disclosable Pecuniary Interests) Regulations 2012 (S.I. 2012/1464) sets out a list of discloseable interests in the Schedule to Regulation 2. Council tax payments or liabilities are not disclosable pecuniary interests but all of the following are (and include those of a spouse or civil partner or any person with whom the member is living as husband or wife, or civil partner):

- Any employment, office, trade, profession or vocation carried on for profit or gain;

- Any payment or provision of any other financial benefit (other than from your council or authority) made or provided within the relevant period in respect of any expenses incurred in carrying out duties as a member, or towards election expenses.

- Any contract between the member (or their spouse or your civil partner or a body in which the member their spouse or civil partner, has a beneficial interest) and the council under which goods or services are to be provided or works are to be executed; and which has not been fully discharged;

- Any beneficial interest in land which the member, or their spouse or civil partner, has within the area of the council;

- Any licence (alone or jointly with others) which the member or their spouse or civil partner, holds to occupy land in the area of the council;

- Any tenancy where the landlord is the council and the member or their spouse or civil partner has a beneficial interest;

- Any beneficial interest which the member or their civil partner or spouse has in securities of a body where (a) that body has a place of business or land in the area of your council or authority; and (b) the total nominal value of the securities/shares exceed certain levels.

The interest simply has to exist to be discloseable, whether or not disclosure might alter the public perception of it and even when the impact of its disclosure is of little relevance to the item being decided. Section 29 requires the monitoring officer of a relevant authority to establish and maintain a register of interests. Section 30 requires a member or a co-opted member of an authority, within 28 days of taking office, to notify the monitoring officer of any disclosable pecuniary interests which that person has at the time of notification. The monitoring officer is required to register such interests.

Section 31 is of most relevance to planning committees. It makes provision for the disclosure of disclosable pecuniary interests which are not registered but which are relevant to matters to be discussed at a meeting of the authority. It also bars a member from participating in any discussion in, or vote on, the matter in relation to which the member has a disclosable pecuniary interest. The duty to disclose and withdraw arises whenever a member attends any meeting, but does not have to be disclosed if it is already registered, though it is good practice to do so. There are limits on the duty of disclosure where there is a risk of violence or intimidation resulting.

If a member has a discloseable pecuniary interest in any matter, they must not participate in any discussion of the matter at the meeting. Where a member has a DPI, it is a criminal offence to fail to register that interest, to fail to disclose it at a meeting unless it is already registered, or to participate on a relevant item of business, unless the member has a dispensation from the authority, or to take any action on the matter as a member of the Executive, other than to refer the matter to another executive member for determination.

Bias and Predetermination

Local authorities and other public bodies have a general duty to act fairly. Public authority decisions that are affected by actual or perceived bias or predetermination are inconsistent with the duty to act fairly. Bias and predetermination tend to be considered together but they are two distinct concepts. When it comes to considering whether or not there has been predetermination there is relevant legislation and a substantial body of case law and both should be considered.

Predetermination: common law

Predetermination is all about the facts. Predetermination occurs when a member participates in a meeting to consider a development proposal with a mind closed to any potential decision and outcome other than that which the member or members in question have already determined to make. Predetermination (if it can be established in all the material facts and circumstances) is always unlawful, in contrast with predisposition – the expression of a point of view or tendency towards deciding one way or another, but with a mind open to other outcomes.

- In *Island Farm* (2007)[17] a claim that a local authority's planning decision was contaminated by predetermination was based on members having a known attitude to the development and one councillor having participated in a protest group. Collins J acknowledged that "Councillors will inevitable be bound to have views on and may well have expressed them

17 R (on the application of Island Farm Development Ltd) v Bridgend County Borough Council [2007] LGR 60

about issues of public interest locally" and that this should not be an automatic disqualification from participation in a planning committee. He was satisfied that the member in question considered the relevant arguments and was "prepared to change his mind" so that there was no apparent predetermination.

- In *Lewis* (2009)[18] a planning application was approved – and the relevant development agreement was completed – immediately before an election. Political control of the local planning authority changed but the new majority group decided to proceed with the development and planning permission was granted. leading to the challenge. Pill LJ noted the position in *Island Farm* and recognised that "Members of a planning committee would be entitled, and indeed expected, to have and to have expressed views on planning issues" and Rix LJ also commented that "Something more is required, something which goes to the appearance of a predetermined, closed mind in the decision-making itself."

- Finally, in *IM Properties Development v Lichfield DC,* a decision of Patterson J in the Planning Court on 18 July 2014, an email from councillor Ian Pritchard (chair of the council's planning committee) sent to Planning Committee Conservative Group members with directions as to how to vote was found to be a 'strongly worded predisposition' and not unlawful predetermination.

18 R(Lewis) v Redcar and Cleveland Borough Council [2008] EWCA Civ 746; [2009] 1 WLR 83.

Predetermination and the Localism Act

Section 25 (1)(a) and (b) of the Localism Act effectively codifies the common law position. It provides that where there has been an allegation of bias or predetermination or there is an issue about the validity of a decision of a relevant authority or circumstances and it is relevant to consider whether any of the decision makers had or appeared to have a closed mind, then (section 25(2)) the decision maker will not be assumed to have had a closed mind solely because they "had previously done anything that directly or indirectly indicated what view the decision maker took, or would or might take". The section does not apply in relation to officers but only to authority members (elected or otherwise) and co-opted members. It preserves some freedom for elected members (but not officers) to express opinions about proposed developments, and even to give an indication of the position they are likely to take when the matter is considered for formal decision-making.

To this extent section 25 is a helpful element of the law relating to predetermination but it does not replace the established body of case law on the same issue which is based on established principles and continues to evolve.

Bias

Bias is much more about perception – and in particular the perception of the public with access to knowledge of the decision-making context.

The legal principles on apparent bias were settled in *Porter v Magill*[19] "The court must first ascertain all the circumstances which have a bearing on the suggestion that the judge was biased. It must then ask whether those circumstances would lead a fair-minded and informed observer to conclude that there was a real possibility, or a real danger, the two being the same, that the tribunal was biased." These fundamental principles have been extensively explored in case law since:

- In Georgiou (2004)[20] Four members of the Planning Committee, three of whom voted in favour of the grant of planning consent, participated in meetings of the local planning authorities Conservation Advisory Group which had considered the merits of the applications prior to them being determined by the Planning Committee. Richards J took the view that this could amount to apparent bias, primarily because the CAG expressed unqualified support for the proposal and the planning committee did not mention "the need for those with dual membership to put on one side the support expressed in the CAG"

- *Berky v Newport*[21]*CC* considered the question of whether the bias of one member would threaten the validity of the decision as a whole. Buxton LJ confirmed that "there is really no reason at all to assume that the mere presence of one member who is biased or has made up his mind in advance must automatically render a decision unlawful.

19 Porter v Magill [2001] UKHL 67; [2002] 2 AC 357

20 Georgiou v London Borough of Enfield and others [2004] EWHC 779

21 *R (Berky) v Newport CC [2012] EWCA Civ 378, [2012] All ER (D) 25 (Apr)*

Such a rule should certainly not be applied when, as in this case, the judge has made a specific finding of fact that the tainted member had no effect on the decision.'

- In *Broadview*[22] an Inspector recommended the grant of planning permission, but was overruled by the Parliamentary Under-Secretary of State. It emerged that the same under-secretary had been lobbied by the local MP both in writing and in a conversation in the parliamentary tea room. Longmore LJ considered that the conversation should not have occurred: "MPs should not, with respect, be in any different position from other interested parties" – but that this did not justify the quashing of the decision.

The most recent and detailed consideration of bias is in the 2018 *Legarde*[23] case that considered the appointment of an Examiner for a neighbourhood plan and the subsequent examination and report. The claimant alleged that Kensington and Chelsea Council was biased in favour of the local neighbourhood forum, giving them privileged access to members and officers and exerting undue influence on the process of examiner selection, the examination process and the examiner's report. Dove J reviewed the relevant cases, including the four included here and established some principles:

---

22 Broadview Energy Developments v Secretary of State for Communities and Local Government and others [2016] EWCA Civ 562.

23 Legard, R (On the Application Of) v The Royal Borough of Kensington and Chelsea [2018] EWHC 32 (Admin) URL: *http://www.bailii.org/ew/cases/EWHC/Admin/2018/32.html*

- The starting point for consideration of bias should be a careful examination of all the facts before the court;

- The test to be applied is whether a fair-minded and informed observer, having considered those facts, would conclude that there was a real possibility of bias;

- The fair-minded observer should be assumed to be "neither unduly suspicious nor complacent", be satisfied that complaints could be justified and would take account of the overall context, including political allegiances and policy positions.

Dove J also noted that planning officers were public officials with a responsibility to "have a listening ear", that the Council had a legal obligation to provide the planning forum with advice and assistance, and that the planning forum's 'protracted and persistent" campaign was legitimate. He considered that it was important for Councillors to remain open to receiving representations as this was 'part and parcel of effective Local Government" and that it was 'perfectly proper' for the council and the examiner to receive ongoing representations from the planning forum during the whole process, even though some of the correspondence was not in the public domain. Dove J concluded that the council's conduct was neither biased nor unfair.

CHAPTER FOUR
REPORTS, REASONS – AND BREXIT…

This final chapter focusses on issues of particular relevance to planning committees: the content of the committee report and the need to give reasons for decisions, as well as some of the legal and procedural issues relating to decision making in planning. It concludes with a review of the current position on consultation – which is always relevant to planning – and Brexit, where relevance is currently unclear.

As well as scrutinising the planning process for evidence of bias and/or predetermination, parties seeking to challenge a local authority's planning decision will look in detail at the committee report, prepared by officers, that frames the recommendation to the committee on how their decision should be made. This is an area where reasonably consistent principles have been established in case law but where those principles are regularly tested.

In *Zurich Assurance*[1] a decision of North Lincolnshire Council was challenged on the basis of deficiencies in the main and addendum reports. Hickinbottom J set out the principles to be applied and they are still relevant:

- In the absence of contrary evidence, it should be inferred that the members followed the reasoning of the report;

---

1 Zurich Assurance Ltd (t/a Threadneedle Property Investments), R (on the application of) v North Lincolnshire Council & Anor [2012] EWHC 3708 (Admin) (20 December 2012) URL: *http://www.bailii.org/ew/cases/EWHC/Admin/2012/3708.html*

- Members of the committee can be assumed to have substantial local and background knowledge including a "working knowledge" of the statutory test.

- Reports should not be interpreted as if they were a statute but rather there should be "a fair reading of the report as a whole."

The most recent and authoritative guidance on the interpretation of planning reports is in the 2017 case of *Mansell v Tonbridge*[2] where the Court of Appeal confirmed that

- reports to committee must be read with reasonable benevolence, and are written for councillors with local knowledge.

- If members followed the officer's recommendation, it can be assumed that they did so on the basis of the advice that he or she gave.

- The court will give a 'fair reading' to the report as a whole and minor errors will be excused.

- The assessment of the report will depend on its "context and circumstances".

- The key question is whether the report "has materially misled the members on a matter bearing upon their decision, and the error has gone uncorrected before the decision was made."

---

2 *Mansell v Tonbridge and Malling BC* [2017] EWCA Civ 1314 at

- Unless there is some distinct and material defect in the officer's advice, the court will not interfere with it.

The Chancellor of the High Court agreed with this position and also commented that

- a minute legalistic dissection of the report was wrong and inappropriate.

- Appeals should not be brought on the basis of a legalistic analysis of the different formulations adopted in a planning officer's report.

- Reports are not, and should not be, written for lawyers.

Recent cases have confirmed this generally relaxed approach to the interpretation of reports. In *KPJR Management Company Ltd v Richmond on Thames*[3] Lang J confirmed that the purpose of a report was to inform the members of the relevant considerations relating to the application and was addressed to those members – who could be expected to have substantial local and background knowledge – and not the world at large. In *Oates v Wealden*[4] the Court of Appeal ruled that "Minor or inconsequential errors are to be distinguished from advice that is significantly or seriously misleading".

However, there are also a number of cases where planning decisions have been quashed because of deficiencies in the way the Committee

3 *R v Mendip DC ex p Fabre* (2000) 80 P&CR 500 at 509).

4 R (on the application of Oates) v Wealden District Council [2018] EWCA Civ 1304

was advised. In *Loader v Rother District Council*[5] the committee considered redevelopment of open space in the setting of a listed building. The Council had attempted to notify the Victorian Society and but did not make any further attempt after an email saying that the individual notified had left the organisation. The Court noted that "the committee was given the impression, wrongly, that the Victorian Society had been consulted and had made no comment on the application, whereas, in truth, the council's attempt to consult them had been abortive…" The court quashed the decision because "the mistake made by the officer in his report was, in its context and circumstances and in its possible consequence, sufficiently misleading to invalidate the committee's decision. In *Watermead Parish Council v Aylesbury Vale*[6] the permission was also quashed because advice the officer gave on the sequential test in relation to flood assessments was "not a true reflection of paragraphs 99 to 104 of the NPPF… the advice the members were given on NPPF policy for the sequential test was in my view defective in law." In *Williams v Powys County Council*[7], the committee considered an application for a wind turbine where the effect of the turbine on the setting of a listed building was highly relevant. The committee was required under section 66(1) of the Listed Buildings Act to "have special regard to the desirability of preserving the building or its setting or any features of special architectural or historic interest which it possesses." The Court noted that "neither the officer's reports to committee nor the county council's decision notice indicated that the county council had in fact performed the duty" and that the absence of relevant advice was "enough to amount to an error of law."

---

5 *R. (on the application of Loader) v Rother District Council* [2016] EWCA Civ 795),

6 *Watermead Parish Council v Aylesbury Vale District Council* [2017] EWCA Civ 152

7 *R. (on the application of Williams) v Powys County Council* [2017] EWCA Civ 427).

The most recent example of deficiencies in the advice to committee is the *Rainbird*[8] case involving the demolition and redevelopment of buildings for commercial and residential purposes. One of the main issues was whether the redevelopment would result in loss of light to neighbouring properties. Howell J confirmed that "The fact that there may be minor mistakes or omissions in an officer's report to a committee does not render any decision based on it unlawful. The question is whether the mistakes or omissions to which I have referred are sufficiently significant or serious as to be material when the report is read as a whole." However the report failed to state the number of properties affected, or the number of rooms that would fail the test. The sunlight and daylight report was misconstrued, the decision to grant planning permission was unlawful and the decision was quashed.

Planning reasons

In the specific context of planning decisions there are discrete requirements relating to planning decisions and also the need for reasons to be recorded for all planning decisions – even those made by planning officers.

Article 35 of the Town and Country Planning (Development Management) Procedure Order 2015[9] requires reasons to be given:

8 Rainbird, R (on the application of) v The Council of the London Borough of Tower Hamlets [2018] EWHC 657 (Admin) URL: *http://www.bailii.org/ew/cases/EWHC/Admin/2018/657.html*

9 http://www.legislation.gov.uk/uksi/2015/595/contents/made

- Where conditions are imposed, reasons for the conditions and – where they are pre-implementation conditions – why they are required at that stage;

- Where permission is refused, including a reference to all relevant development plan policies;

- Where a Direction has been issued so that permission would not normally be granted, reasons why an exception has been made in this case.

In addition, regulation 24(1)(c) of the Environmental Impact Regulations requires that where an EIA application is determined by a local planning authority, the authority must inform the public of the decision and make available for public inspection a statement, containing… (ii) the main reasons and considerations on which the decision is based including, if relevant, information about the participation of the public;"

The principles regulating the need to give reasons for a grant of a permission were comprehensively explored by the Supreme Court in the 2018 case of CPRE v Dover DC[10] The proposal was for a retirement village on a site designated as a scheduled monument and within the Kent Downs Area of Outstanding Natural Beauty. The initial report was referred to as a 'remarkable' document and recommended approval, subject to the exclusion of a 2ha safeguarded area. This proposal was resisted by the applicant and members voted in favour of the original scheme. A later vote approved the decision to grant permission on the basis of a further report updating members

10 https://www.supremecourt.uk/cases/uksc-2016-0188.html

on the terms of the 106 agreement and permission was granted when the agreement was completed.

The initial challenge was made on a number of grounds including the lack of reasons for the second decision, and dismissed, and the Supreme Court granted permission to appeal in order to consider that issue. They confirmed that while there was no general common law duty to give reasons for decisions, in some circumstances it could be required even in the absence of a statutory requirement: "Although planning law is a creature of statute, the proper interpretation of the statute is underpinned by general principles, properly referred to as derived from the common law."

In this particular case their Lordships ruled that reasons were required because of:

- The high profile and controversial nature of the proposal;
- The 'admitted breach' of the requirement to give reasons under the EIA regulations;
- The departure from AONB policies
- The lack of clarity as to how members voted and why "there is no indication of how or why the members felt able, without further investigation, to reject the view of their own advisers that the viability of the scheme need not be threatened, and indeed could be enhanced."

The Supreme Court Concluded that "these points were not merely incidental, but were fundamental to the officers' support for the amended scheme... This is a case where the defect in reasons goes to the heart of the justification for the permission, and undermines its validity."

In the light of this decision, where a decision is controversial or complex, or involves a departure from development plan or national policies, it is recommended that full reasons are given to avoid the risk of a challenge on this basis.

Planning Decisions

There is often some confusion, especially when calculating the risk of a judicial review, what the date of the actual decision is – but the case of *Burkett v Hammersmith and Fulham*[11] confirms that it is the date of the permission and not the resolution that is to be considered. In this case the committee resolution was issued on 15 September 1999, the application for permission to bring a judicial review was submitted on 6th April and planning permission was granted on 12 May 2000. The House of Lords confirmed that "time runs from the date of the grant and not from the date of the resolution. The resolution itself created no legal rights because it was subject to (i) there being no call in decision by the Secretary of State and (ii) completion of a section 106 agreement. Until these conditions were satisfied and the planning permission itself was granted, there were no rights or obligations between the local authority, the developer and the affected individuals and the resolution could be revoked.

11 London Borough of Hammersmith and Fulham and Others, R v. [2002] UKHL 23

However, once the permission has been issued it cannot be revoked – except by a formal action to quash made by a person with standing or – in the case of an error – by the local authority itself. This was confirmed in *Carrol v South Somerset* in 2008[12] involving an application for residential development. Permission was granted subject to confirmation from the Secretary of State that call in was not required. The committee resolved to grant permission subject to referral to the Secretary of State and to the completion of section 106 agreement. The Secretary of State subsequently confirmed that the Council could deal with the matter and the planning officer authorised the issue of the decision notice, without completion of the section 106 agreement.

The time for bringing a judicial review expired and only at that point did the council realise that a mistake had been made. The Council invited the applicant to agree that a mistake had been made and invite the court to grant a declaration to that effect. The applicant claimed that the permission was valid. The Council took the view that, in the absence of a specific consent, it was necessary to seek judicial review of the decision and to have it quashed.

Collins J confirmed that the officer actions were well within their delegated authority and so the grant of the permission was valid, but that the only sensible construction of the committee resolution, and the minutes of the meeting, was that the section 106 agreement should have been in place prior to the permission being granted. He confirmed that "in circumstances such as this the correct course is to do what has been done, namely to have a senior member of the Council, in this case the leader who would normally be the appro-

12 Carroll, R (on the application of) v Luken Beck Partnership Ltd & Anor [2008] EWHC 104 (Admin) (14 January 2008)

priate person, to take the proceedings in his name and thereby to sort out the situation."

Collins J did not accept that there had been any prejudice to the applicant or to Wimpey Homes, the subsequent owner of the land: " the reality is that they were the recipients of an unlawful planning permission and therefore they had nothing on which they could properly rely."

Consultation

Engagement generally, and consultation in particular, are important considerations in any planning decision. In many cases consultation requirements are set out in regulations and it is simply a matter of complying with those requirements – though as the *Loader v Rother* case demonstrates, there should be full compliance with them. There are other circumstances where a decision is to be made in a planning context but it is either not clear whether consultation is required (such as approving a construction programme for a very controversial development) or it is not clear what the consultation requirements are (such as the initial stages of a neighbourhood plan). In both sets of circumstances it is important to be aware of the common law context and the guidance available.

It is important to remember that even where there is no formal requirement to consult, the circumstances might have created a situation where parties affected by the decision have a 'legitimate expectation" that they will be consulted.

This has recently been considered by Mr Justice Dove[13] in relation to a challenge to a Written Ministerial Statement on neighbourhood planning. He acknowledged that a legitimate expectation of consultation could be created by an express representation that there would be one or where there as established practice in relation to such documents generally. Mr Justice Dove went on to conclude in this case no legitimate expectation of consultation existed because 1) the evidence did not establish that there had been an unequivocal assurance on the basis of practice that a WMS in relation to national planning policy for housing would not be issued without prior consultation and 2) on at least two previous occasions an WMS was issued without consultation.

Legitimate expectation was also considered in *Kebbel Developments*[14] which considered was whether the Council should have consulted on its decision to depart from the examiner's recommendations when modifying the provisions of a neighbourhood plan. In this case there was a particular difficulty because the regulations setting out the definition of "prescribed persons" for consultation purposes were not in force at the time the council took its decision. The Court considered whether a duty to consult arose in this circumstance and began by distinguishing between general procedural fairness in the treatment of individuals and the more general concept of the need for public participation in a public authority's decision-making process. The court went on to confirm that:

---

13 Richborough Estates Ltd v Secretary of State for Housing, Communities And Local Government [2018] EWHC 33 (Admin) (12 January 2018) URL: *http://www.bailii.org/ew/cases/EWHC/Admin/2018/33.html*

14 Kebbell Developments Ltd v Leeds City Council [2018] EWCA Civ 450 (14 March 2018) URL: *http://www.bailii.org/ew/cases/EWCA/Civ/2018/450.html*

- A public authority duty to consult can arise from statue and/or delegated legislation

- where there is a legitimate expectation of such consultation, arising from an interest which is held to be sufficient to found such an expectation, or from some promise or practice of consultation.

- There is no general common law duty to consult persons who may be affected by a measure before it is adopted,

In this case there was no breach of the general requirements of "procedural fairness" or any "legitimate expectation" to be consulted. In the circumstances the court ruled that there was "neither a statutory duty of consultation nor ... any legitimate expectation which would be the source of such a duty.

In terms of consultation generally the most important considerations are the common law principles that apply to all public consultations established in caselaw[15]and referred to as the *Gunning Principles*:

- **Consultation must take place when the proposal is still at a formative stage:** This principle does not mean that the decision-maker has to consult on all possible options of achieving a particular objective. A decision-maker can consult on a 'preferred option', and even a 'decision in principle', so long as its mind is genuinely open – '*to have an open mind does not mean an empty mind.*'

15 R v London Borough of Brent ex parte Gunning

- **Sufficient reasons must be put forward for the proposal to allow for intelligent consideration and response:** Consultees should be made aware of the basis on which a proposal for consultation has been considered and will thereafter be considered. Those consulted should be aware of the criteria that will be applied when considering proposals and what factors will be considered 'decisive' or 'of substantial importance' at the end of the process.

- **Adequate time must be given for consideration and response:** Unless statutory time requirements are prescribed, there is no necessary time frame within which the consultation must take place. The decision-maker may adopt a policy as to the necessary time-frame (e.g. Cabinet Office guidance, or compact with the voluntary sector), and if it wishes to depart from that policy it should have a good reason for doing so. Otherwise, it may be guilty of a breach of a legitimate expectation that the policy will be adhered to. The Government tends to use 3, 4 or 6 week periods depending on what it is consulting on. It is an accepted convention that, were possible, the decision maker should avoid holiday weekends and times when people are likely to be away such as the summer.

- **The product of consultation must be conscientiously taken into account:** If the decision-maker does not properly consider the material produced by the consultation, then it can be accused of having made up its mind; or of failing to take into account a relevant consideration.

The principles of the Aarhus Convention in relation to Access to Information, Public Participation in Decision-Making and Access to Justice in Environmental Matters are also relevant here. Article 7 of the Aarhus Convention requires parties to the Convention to make appropriate practical and or other provisions for public participation in relation to plans and programmes relating to the environment. Article 6(8) provides specifically that "Each party shall ensure that in the decision due account is taken of the outcome of the public parti - cipation."

Consultation requirements were considered in the *Maldon* case[16] involving the approval of an application for a reserved matters consent. Mr Justice Howell commented that "whether or not con- sultation is a legal requirement, if it is embarked on, it must be carried out properly by a public authority and the applicable prin- ciples of fairness are no different from those that apply if the consultation is statutory." He went on to rule that "in order for any consultation to be fairly conducted, that those consulted know on what they are being consulted". Failure to consult to this standard was enough on its own to invalidate the decision in this case.

The most prominent recent case involving consultation involved a challenge by 'Talk Fracking' to the Government's adoption of the new National Planning Policy Framework in July 2018[17] Ground 4, was the contention that the government failed to carry out a lawful consultation exercise on the Framework revisions. Dove J noted that the common law duty of procedural fairness applied in this context

---

16 Pearl, R (on the application of) v Maldon District Council & Anor [2018[EWHC 212

17 Stephenson v Secretary of State for Housing and Communities and Local Government [2019] EWHC 519 (Admin) (06 March 2019) URL: *http://www.bailii.org/ew/cases/EWHC/Admin/2019/519.html*

and endorsed the *Gunning* principles commenting that "It is hard to see how any of his four suggested requirements could be rejected or indeed improved." He noted that where a detailed response to a consultation was not properly considered the consultation process could be "so unfair as to be unlawful." He ruled that:

- In relation to a consultation process the purpose of the documentation is to secure the engagement of the public and their contribution to the decision-making process on the issues which they are to be led to consider are the subject matter of the decision-making process, that is to say the issues within the scope of the decision-making process.

- Paragraph 209(a) of the Framework was simply a "cut and paste" of the previous Written Ministerial Statement on Fracking and that " there was no interest in reviewing or re-evaluating the substance of the policy of the 2015 WMS, or listening to any consultation engaged with the merits of the policy or the evidential and scientific issues associated with it."

- No 'reasonable reader' could have known from the consultation document or the official response to the consultation that in reality the policy contained in paragraph 204(a) of the consultation draft of the Framework was outside the scope of the consultation.

- This element of the consultation was therefore legally flawed because the Government "had a closed mind as to the content of the policy and was not undertaking the consultation at a formative stage."

- In addition the Government "did not conscientiously consider the fruits of the consultation exercise"

He concluded that "the consultation exercise involved breaches of the Sedley principles which are the requirements for a fair and lawful consultation exercise…the consultation on the draft revised Framework paragraph 204(a) was so flawed in its design and processes as to be unlawful."

Another general point worth noting in relation to consultation requirements is the case of Kendall v Rochford District Council [18] which was a rare example of the courts considering the validity of electronic consultation for complying with statutory requirements. The judge commented that sole reliance on a website consultation "was not an effective means of consulting the public" and that "members of the public – certainly the inhabitants of Rayleigh – would not have been aware that consultation under the SEA regulations was taking place unless they happened to have heard about it by chance." He went on to refer to this as a "basic failure to comply with regulation 13… I cannot accept that the council could properly consult the general public under the SEA regulations in that way." It is worth bearing in mind that although the general public now gets its information mostly through electronic methods and social media, the judiciary is likely to take a traditional and strict approach.

European considerations and Brexit

The two cases referred to in Chapter 2 involving the Habitats Directive demonstrate that third parties are increasingly ready to take

18 Kendall v Rochford District Council & Ano [2014] EWHC 3866 (Admin)

their concerns to the European Courts and that those courts are ready and able to make rulings that contradict the approach of the English courts. It is an area where it is a good idea to err on the side of caution when considering how a Directive should be complied with.

One of the many uncertainties connected to these European requirements is the effect of Brexit. Any trading relationships with EU members will depend on the UK demonstrating that its legislation is equivalent to that of the EU in all areas including environmental regulation.

It is unlikely that Brexit will signal a simple dismantling of the EIA regime altogether. Indeed the immediate effects will be minimal as regulations have been laid[19] amending the EIA Regulations and associated legislation to ensure that preserve EU law within domestic law or convert it into UK law from exit day onwards, though there will be no reciprocity with EU member states. Other regulations[20] have been made to reflect changes necessary to implement the 'People over Wind" case along with corresponding amendments to the Framework.

The future looks less certain. The Government published the draft Environment (Principles and Governance) bill on 19th December 2018 including the creation of an *independent body – the Office for Environmental Protection or OEP – which will scrutinise environmental law and the government's environmental improvement plan,*

19 The Environmental Assessments and Miscellaneous Planning (Amendment) (EU Exit) Regulations 2018/1232

20 The Conservation of Habitats and Species and Planning (Various Amendments) (England and Wales) Regulations 2018/1307

investigate complaints on environmental law and take enforcement action on breaches of that law. The wider Environment Bill is expected to be introduced in the second Parliamentary session in 2019. However a number of concerns have already been raised[21] in relation to the independence of the new body, its funding arrangements, the independence of its member, and its enforcement powers and the exclusion of climate change mitigation (greenhouse gas emissions) from the scope of the definition of environmental law.

21 https://publications.parliament.uk/pa/cm201719/cmselect/cmenvfru/1893/1893.pdf

'A Practical Guide to Licensing Law for Commercial Property Lawyers' by Niall McCann & Richard Williams
'A Practical Guide to Adoption for Family Lawyers' by Graham Pegg
'Essential Motor Finance Law for the Busy Practitioner' by Richard Humphreys
'A Practical Guide to Industrial Disease Claims' by Andrew Mckie & Ian Skeate
'A Practical Guide to the Law of Armed Conflict' by Jo Morris & Libby Anderson
'A Practical Guide to Redundancy' by Philip Hyland
'A Practical Guide to Vicarious Liability' by Mariel Irvine
'A Practical Guide to Claims Arising from Delays in Diagnosing Cancer' by Bella Webb
'A Practical Guide to Applications for Landlord's Consent and Variation of Leases' by Mark Shelton
'A Practical Guide to Relief from Sanctions Post-Mitchell and Denton' by Peter Causton
'Butler's Equine Tax Planning: 2nd Edition' by Julie Butler
'A Practical Guide to Equity Release for Advisors' by Paul Sams
'A Practical Guide to Unlawful Eviction and Harassment' by Stephanie Lovegrove
'A Practical Guide to the Law Relating to Food' by Ian Thomas
'A Practical Guide to the Ending of Assured Shorthold Tenancies' by Elizabeth Dwomoh
'A Practical Guide to Financial Services Claims' by Chris Hegarty
'The Law of Houses in Multiple Occupation: A Practical Guide to HMO Proceedings' by Julian Hunt
'A Practical Guide to Unlawful Eviction and Harassment' by Stephanie Lovegrove
'A Practical Guide to Solicitor and Client Costs' by Robin Dunne
'A Practical Guide to Wrongful Conception, Wrongful Birth and Wrongful Life Claims' by Rebecca Greenstreet
'Occupiers, Highways and Defective Premises Claims: A Practical Guide Post-Jackson – 2nd Edition' by Andrew Mckie
'A Practical Guide to Financial Ombudsman Service Claims' by Adam Temple & Robert Scrivenor

'A Practical Guide to the Law of Enfranchisement and Lease Extension' by Paul Sams
'A Practical Guide to Marketing for Lawyers – 2nd Edition' by Catherine Bailey & Jennet Ingram
'A Practical Guide to Advising Schools on Employment Law' by Jonathan Holden
'Certificates of Lawful Use and Development: A Guide to Making and Determining Applications' by Bob Mc Geady & Meyric Lewis
'A Practical Guide to the Law of Dilapidations' by Mark Shelton
'A Practical Guide to the 2018 Jackson Personal Injury and Costs Reforms' by Andrew Mckie
'A Guide to Consent in Clinical Negligence Post-Montgomery' by Lauren Sutherland QC
'A Practical Guide to Running Housing Disrepair and Cavity Wall Claims: 2nd Edition' by Andrew Mckie & Ian Skeate
'A Practical Guide to Digital and Social Media Law for Lawyers' by Sherree Westell
'A Practical Guide to Holiday Sickness Claims – 2nd Edition' by Andrew Mckie & Ian Skeate
'A Practical Guide to Elderly Law' by Justin Patten
'Arguments and Tactics for Personal Injury and Clinical Negligence Claims' by Dorian Williams
'A Practical Guide to QOCS and Fundamental Dishonesty' by James Bentley
'A Practical Guide to Drone Law' by Rufus Ballaster, Andrew Firman, Eleanor Clot
'Practical Mediation: A Guide for Mediators, Advocates, Advisers, Lawyers, and Students in Civil, Commercial, Business, Property, Workplace, and Employment Cases' by Jonathan Dingle with John Sephton
'A Comparative Guide to Standard Form Construction and Engineering Contracts' by Jon Close
'A Practical Guide to Compliance for Personal Injury Firms Working With Claims Management Companies' by Paul Bennett
'A Practical Guide to the Landlord and Tenant Act 1954: Commercial Tenancies' by Richard Hayes & David Sawtell
'A Practical Guide to Psychiatric Claims in Personal Injury' by Liam Ryan
'A Practical Guide to Dog Law for Owners and Others' by Andrea Pitt

Printed in Great Britain
by Amazon

85506664R00061